P9-DGU-347

Signs of Hope in the City

Robert Linthicum, editor

MARC

121 East Huntington Drive, Monrovia, California 91016-3400 USA

Signs of Hope in the City

Robert C. Linthicum, Editor

ISBN 0-912552-95-6

Published by MARC, a division of World Vision International, 121
East Huntington Drive, Monrovia, California 91016-3400, U.S.A.

Printed in the United States of America. Editors and page layout:
Ken Graff and Edna Valdez. Cover design: Richard Sears.

All Scripture quotations, unless otherwise indicated or when they
appear in quoted material, are taken from the Revised Standard Ver-
sion of the Bible, copyright 1946, 1952, 1971 by the Division of
Christian Education of the National Council of Churches of Christ in
the USA. Used by permission.

CONTENTS

APPENDIXES

CREDITS

The International Urban Ministry Network (IUMN) is an informational Christian body of urban church leaders, pastors, denominational and mission agency executives, urban ministry trainers and missiologists from the major cities of all continents and from the five major ecclesiastical traditions, defined as Orthodox, Roman Catholic, conciliar Protestant, evangelical and Pentecostal/charismatic.

Robert Linthicum, editor of this book, is executive director of Partners in Urban Transformation and a convener of the Ruschlikon Consultation. He is current moderator of the IUMN and international coordinator for IUMN's International Urban Ministry Congress, scheduled for Nairobi, Kenya in November 1996. From 1985 to 1995, Linthicum headed the Office of Urban Advance, an international urban community organizing and training network associated with World Vision International. Linthicum is a minister of the Presbyterian Church (USA), having served city churches for 25 years before joining World Vision International. He is the author of *City of God, City of Satan: An Urban Biblical Theology* and *Empowering the Poor*.

PREFACE

Signs of Hope in the City not only breaks new urban ministry and theological ground, it also invites the reader into the conversation between some of Christianity's outstanding leaders in urban ministry. The papers contained in this book began as presentations made at two important urban ministry events. On August 18-23, 1991, Roman Catholics, evangelicals, Orthodox, conciliar Protestants and Pentecostals from around the world gathered in the village of Ruschlikon, near Zurich, for a consultation seeking urban ministry commonality. On July 25-30, 1993, representatives from the Ruschlikon event gathered in Sheffield, England. At both events, papers on theologies, missiology and the history of urban ministry were presented and received response. The best of these papers are presented in edited form here in *Signs of Hope in the City*.

It was the privilege of International Urban Associates and the Office of Urban Advance of World Vision International to sponsor the Ruschlikon event. Out of Ruschlikon grew the International Urban Ministry Network, about which you will hear further in this book.

In the spirit of Ruschlikon and Sheffield, I commend to you *Signs of Hope in the City*. I know you will find it as stimulating reading as I found it insightful to listen to these presentations.

Ray Bakke
International Urban Associates

1

INTRODUCTION

O n August 18-23, 1991, an event without precedents occurred. During that week, 44 grassroots urban ministry leaders from all major ecclesiastical traditions and from around the world gathered at the Baptist Theological Seminary in Ruschlikon (Zurich), Switzerland. These pastors, community organizers, teachers and mission agency executives came from the Roman Catholic, Orthodox, conciliar Protestant, evangelical and Pentecostal traditions. They came from all over the world— from urban slums and squatter settlements in the Philippines and Ethiopia, India and Mexico, South Africa and the United Kingdom, from highly effective urban churches in Australia and the former Yugoslavia, Kenya and France, New Zealand and Romania, from academic communities and mission agencies in the United States and Egypt, India and Canada, Switzerland and Costa Rica. The purpose of this consultation was stated in a later reflection by one of its participants, Grant McClung of the Church of God:

> Our objective in gathering would be to look for signs of hope and by sharing about the work of God's people in the city, discern what the Spirit is doing all over the urban world. Out of such sharing, we may begin to determine some means by which the whole church can think together about the city and carry out mission in the light of those common perceptions.

2

Those signs of hope surrounded the participants in this gathering. They felt strongly the grief and pain of their division and brokenness as they spoke about their differing urban ministry experiences. We discovered, as the closing press release of the consultation stated, that we are much closer than we could have imagined, as we have heard the convictions of our traditions affirmed by members of other traditions.

As a result of the growing commitment of these Roman Catholic, Orthodox, Protestant, evangelical and Pentecostal Christians to each other and to the future of urban missions in an increasingly urban world, the consultation participants pledged to each other:

> It is important for the future of urban mission to find concrete ways of cooperation, to honor, trust and love one another for the sake of Jesus Christ, who said that the world may believe that you have sent me.

That commitment resulted in the formation of an ongoing organization—International Urban Ministry Network (IUMN). The IUMN has continued the spirit of Ruschlikon by maintaining conversation between these consultant participants, by bringing a steadily-growing number of urban ministry practitioners into the network, by conducting continuing theological and missiological reflection, by publications and by planning an International Urban Ministry Congress for November 24-December 1, 1996, in Nairobi, Kenya. This Congress will gather urban Christians from all major church traditions throughout the world united in solidarity with the world's poor to sound a call and to create strategies to make urban ministry the church's priority in the twenty-first century.

On July 25-30, 1993, another urban ministry gathering was held in Sheffield, England, which called together 14 of the Ruschlikon 44. That meeting of the IUMN Steering, Publications and Theological Committees was held primarily to make future plans for the IUMN. But much time was also spent in theological and missiological discussion.

At both the Ruschlikon and Sheffield meetings, papers were presented on a wide spectrum of urban ministry concerns. The impact of these papers, when considered together, is one that offers signs of hope to all of those involved in urban ministry. We were struck with the depth and breadth of theological reflection, and with an understanding of what the history of urban ministry and the context of the city can provide us. But particularly we were profoundly moved by the wide variety, creativity and effectiveness of urban ministry occurring in all five traditions and at all levels of church government.

We would like to share with you from these papers, so that they can become signs of hope to you as they were to us. We have gathered into this book highlights and summaries of some of the papers presented at both the Ruschlikon and Sheffield events. Several of the papers also had formal responses, so we have included summaries of them as well. These papers will be considered in three categories: theology, history and context, and missiology.

Enjoy! And let your hopes for the city and its church once again begin to soar.

A Time to Talk:
The Ruschlikon Movement

A Time to Talk: The Ruschlikon Movement

This chapter was written by Robert Linthicum, the editor of this book.

Has not the time come for all leaders in Christian urban ministry to talk to one another?

This question emerged in 1989 as Raymond Fung, a leader in Protestant ministry among unrepresented workers and the poor in Hong Kong, was talking with Kenneth Luscombe, a Baptist pastor involved in community organizing and church renewal in Melbourne, Australia.

In his ministry in inner-city Melbourne, Luscombe had for several years felt unease at what appeared to him and his colleagues to be an urban mission movement that seemed to be as diverse as the number of people in urban ministry. Each organization or group seemed to be doing what was right in its own eyes.

In 1989, after joining the staff of the Office of Urban Advance, World Vision International, Luscombe discovered that what he had seen in his local experience was also true of the urban church internationally. His sense of a somewhat formless urban universe with diverse and unconnected constellations circling around one or another major urban luminary was both correct and universally felt. There needed to be some means that would bring these luminaries together to think more collaboratively regarding urban ministry, even if it meant leaping theological traditions and ecclesiastical systems.

Luscombe shared his concern with me, his colleague in the Office of Urban Advance. We decided he should broach the topic with Raymond Fung on an upcoming trip through Geneva, where Fung was then secretary of the evangelism unit of the World Council of Churches.

At their meeting, Fung and Luscombe began talking about the whole field of urban ministry. They reflected on the innovative urban work occurring in both the evangelical and the conciliar (ecumenical or mainline Protestant) traditions.

Suddenly, Fung spoke what was on both their minds. What a tragedy it was that the body of Christ was learning so little from the many people involved in urban ministry and yet kept separate from each other by their differences in theology, ecclesiology and liturgies! What a great boon it would be if leaders could set aside—even for a moment—the differences that separate in order to discover together the love of Christ and city, a love that could bind them together! Had not the time come, Fung mused, for leaders from the primary traditions of Christianity to begin learning from one another about living out the gospel in the city?

Luscombe was greatly encouraged to hear another urban leader express his deep concern. He returned to his office in the United States to share that moment with me. The seeds of an international movement had been sown.

That movement became known as the International Urban Ministry Network (IUMN). It includes urban Christians from every continent—priests and lay urban workers, biblical scholars and slum workers, denominational and agency urban executives, pastors and teachers, evangelists and community organizers, teachers of urban ministry and parachurch urban staff. Most importantly, it includes leaders from the full spectrum of the Christian church.

IUMN is not an organization or institution. Nor is it a program or series of projects. Rather, it is Christians—in both so-called high and low positions—who see themselves as called to a ministry in the city. They come together to share and learn from one another, to celebrate and worship together, to better discern what God is doing all over the urban world, to be open to receive God's gifts for the renewing of their lives and ministries and to develop ongoing networks, resources, support mechanisms and associations for carrying out the mission of Christ in the city.

IUMN was born at a 1991 conference in Ruschlikon, a small town on the outskirts of Zurich, Switzerland.

Revolutions in Ruschlikon and Russia

Some decisions are historic because of their content. Others are historic because of the way external events invade and transform them. Both elements were found in the August 18-23, 1991, International Urban Consultation that became known as the Ruschlikon experience.

On the first day of the consultation, news reached us of an attempted coup occurring in the Soviet Union. This historic event foreshadowed the collapse of that empire. At Ruschlikon were three delegates from the Soviet hegemony. The entire delegation gathered around the lone television set, viewing the night watch by thousands of students and Christians in front of the Soviet White House and Russian Palace. None of us will forget the scene of one of our number pacing back and forth in front of the television set as incident after incident unfolded.

We gathered for prayer with our brothers from Eastern Europe. We sat in little groups, talking into the night. Did the coup attempt mean the end of the emerging political springtime in Russia, still another return to a Soviet police state? Or was it the dawning of a new day?

By the next morning, it was clear that the long night of Soviet control was over. The coup had collapsed. A shaken and surprisingly subdued Mikhail Gorbachev was returned to power. The heroes of the moment were Boris

Yeltsin and the Russian people. We had seen the beginning of the end of the Soviet empire.

We all gathered to praise God for this miraculous intervention in human history. Suddenly, our task of enabling God's people of every continent, political persuasion and ecclesiastical tradition to work together for the good of the world's cities took on an immediacy and imperative quality none of us could have anticipated. In such a shifting and insecure world, only the worldwide body of Christ could offer a firm hope for the city.

Internal events had also profoundly shaped the Ruschlikon consultation. Ken Luscombe had returned from his 1989 meeting with Raymond Fung to share with me and with Raymond Bakke the vision of the primary Christian traditions learning from one another how to live out the gospel in the world's cities. Bakke, the executive director of the International Urban Associates, the Lausanne senior associate for world-class cities and international spokesperson for evangelical urban ministry, arranged for a further meeting between Fung, Luscombe, myself and himself in April 1990. A proposal emerged for a consultation to bring together urban Christian leaders.

By March 1991, Bakke and I had invited pivotal urban clergy and laity from the five major Christian traditions (defined as conciliar Protestant, Roman Catholic, Orthodox, evangelical and Pentecostal/charismatic). Leaders from throughout the world were asked to come together frankly acknowledging our ideological and theological differences, but with a common commitment to share out of our respective experiences and conceptual frameworks, and thus learn from each other.

Responding to this invitation, forty-four participants and spouses from twenty different denominations or affiliations gathered in August 1991 at the Baptist Theological

Seminary in Ruschlikon, Switzerland (see Appendix Two for a list of those attending). The forty-four representatives and spouses represented sixteen nations and fourteen languages or mother tongues. They were thirty-five men and nine women, eighteen Protestants, eleven evangelicals, seven Pentecostals and charismatics, five Orthodox and three Roman Catholics.

The consultation focused on five themes:

❖ Learning from the history of urban mission
❖ Reflecting theologically on urban missions
❖ Examining the developing urban context
❖ Exploring how our respective traditions have sought to do ministry in these contexts
❖ Wrestling with three questions:
  • What have we heard?
  • What shall we do?
  • How and when shall we do it?

Michael Eastman of Frontier Youth Trust, London, observed that the consultation actually went through four phases: listening and learning, relationship-building (when we learned to both trust and confront one another), grappling with commonly identified issues (about which there was significant agreement) and decision-making (which included setting strategies). Eastman said that in his experience, most conferences can handle only two such transitions.

We disagreed and fought at times, but nobody walked out. By the end of the event, we participants had been knit into a cohesive body committed to one another while acknowledging significant differences.

The results of Ruschlikon

The following statement was drafted and amended on the final day of the consultation. This declaration

develops a common statement of conclusions, direction
and mission from the members of all traditions present:

> We, members of major Christian traditions, Protes-
> tant, Catholic, Orthodox, evangelical and Pente-
> costal, from 16 countries and different social,
> political and economic contexts, met at the Baptist
> Theological Seminary in Ruschlikon, Switzerland,
> 18-23 August 1991, to share with one another our
> different mission experiences and to discover com-
> mon insights.
>
> During our meeting we strongly felt the grief and
> pain of our brokenness and division as we tried to
> find a common language in our approach to mis-
> sion in the city.
>
> Listening to one another, however, we discovered
> that we are much closer than we could have imag-
> ined, as we have heard the convictions of our own
> traditions affirmed by members of other traditions.
>
> We expressed our common commitment to pro-
> claim Jesus as Lord and to study the Bible as the liv-
> ing word of God, to witness in our cities to the
> Father, Son and Holy Spirit and to God's kingdom
> by word, prayer, community and worship, by our
> transformed lives, by our service to people and by
> our struggle for justice.
>
> We listened with respect to the accounts of different
> ways of working, as evangelists, community orga-
> nizers, providers of services, church leaders and as
> advocates for the marginalized and oppressed. Our
> conference was enriched by the presence of a mem-
> ber of another living faith.
>
> Finally, we agreed that it is important for the future
> of urban mission to find concrete ways of coopera-
> tion, to honor, trust and love one another for the

sake of Jesus Christ, that the world may believe that
you have sent me.

Besides the statement, six other actions were taken
by the participants in the consultation to continue the
Ruschlikon movement.

First, continuity would be maintained by a steering
committee drawn from all five traditions and from each
continent. This group of twelve has met twice since
Ruschlikon, at Sheffield, England on July 25-30, 1993,
and in Chicago, USA on April 7-8, 1994.

Second, a report on the consultation would be published. This book is that report, including its theological,
historical and missiological reflections. The Steering
Committee later added the reflections of the Sheffield
meeting to that report.

Third, a second international consultation or congress would be planned. The purpose of this second
international event would be to resource and sustain the
urban agenda of the respective traditions and to provide
means for cross-fertilization of the pivotal urban ministries and players of those traditions. A committee was
appointed from among the Ruschlikon participants to
develop a second international consultation. The present
date for the international congress is November 24-
December 1, 1996 and will be held in Nairobi, Kenya. It
is planned for 300 delegates, 150 of whom will be from
African cities.

Fourth, the development of a traveling institute for
advanced urban training would be explored. The purpose for such an institute would be to offer advanced
reflection, debate and thinking about urban ministry—an
ingredient missing from many training centers today. It
was decided that the potential of such an institute could
be explored by holding an advanced reflection event

immediately before or after the Nairobi congress. A committee was formed to bring such an institute into being.

Fifth, publications would be produced by a committee appointed from among the Ruschlikon participants. The publications would disseminate the consultation's mission statement, proceedings and reflections. Also, the Office of Urban Advance, World Vision International, was asked to create and maintain an international directory.

Sixth, each participant would take responsibility for developing and maintaining linkages with urban ministers, pastors and leaders of all five traditions. We pledged ourselves to network-building at local, national and regional levels and to the task of maintaining and developing relationships among delegates and wider network links.

At the continental divide

The abortive coup against Gorbachev was a foreshadowing of the death of the Soviet Union, the collapse of the cold war and the birth of a post-communist world. Watching the people in Red Square stopping the tanks of the Soviet army and maintaining a candlelight vigil was in itself awesome and mind-boggling. But the seismic forces at work behind their gathering—forces that would destroy one world and birth another—were of far greater consequence and yet invisible. As we sat in solidarity as a Christian urban community with our Eastern European brothers watching this drama played out before our eyes on television, we all sensed that we were watching the birth of something we had never before experienced and of which we could have only vaguely dreamt.

The same could be said for our experience as urban Christians at Ruschlikon. We were, indeed, a varied group of people differentiated by race, nationality, culture, language, traditions, denominations, gender and ministry. But we gathered with a common commitment to Christ and a common love of the city. We met, we listened, we argued, we defined common causes, we worked out issues, we drew up a strategy, decided courses of action and established mechanisms to carry out those plans. We also laughed a great deal, supported those going through the terror of events over which they had no control, took long walks together, sun-bathed, gathered for sustaining worship and prayed and studied together. And out of those events came the firm pledge to work for the day when urban ministry would become a primary agenda of the whole church—Roman Catholic, Orthodox, Protestant, evangelical, and Pentecostal— throughout the whole world.

Did we accomplish it? Were seismic forces created— shock waves that would eventually birth a church committed to the city and the liberation of the poor? Or was Ruschlikon, as Michael Eastman so graphically wrote, simply destined to be a footnote in future D.Min. dissertations? Only the future holds the answer to that question.

Ken and Joy Luscombe had been students at the Baptist Theological Seminary at Ruschlikon from 1977 through 1980. It was they who had recommended Ruschlikon as the venue for this historic consultation. Following the event, they took my wife and me on a trip into the Swiss Alps to see some of their favorite spots.

We visited many little Swiss towns, picnicked in a delightful Alpine meadow, shivered on snow-clad peaks and stood awestruck before immense mountain vistas. But what struck me the most was our visit to an unusual little chapel.

We had driven for several hours up tortuous, winding roads as the scenery changed from pine trees to Alpine tundra and, finally, to bare rock and snow. It was incredibly cold and windy. Suddenly Ken pulled to the side of the road and declared, "We're here!" We got out of the car, our breath ripped from our lungs by the biting wind. We could barely see what lay in the direction of Ken's pointing hand because of the driving snow. But then the wind abated ever so slightly and we could see on the mountainside above us what appeared to be a small stone hut. We began trudging toward it and, as we neared it, I could see that it was a small, rough-hewn chapel.

We stepped inside the chapel, into the cold but quiet clarity of a house of worship on the roof of the world. After standing in awe for a few minutes, we stepped back through the door—and with my back to the church, I could now see what was not observable when we approached the chapel. We were atop Europe's continental divide. On one side of us lay the twisted road we had followed to get up here, disappearing like a ribbon back into the world out of which we had struggled. And on the other side of us lay the ridge of the mountain and the road heading down into the warm and welcoming climes of Italy.

Could not this chapel be for us a parable of the Ruschlikon experience, as the church travels into the unknown world of an urban future?

Theologies of Urban Mission

Tomorrow is Our Permanent Address: Toward a Trinitarian Theology for the City

From a presentation by Benigno Beltran, a priest of the Society of the Divine Word and pastor of the Church of the Risen Christ in the Smokey Mountain slum of Manila, the Philippines. A response is given by Ioan Sauca of the Romanian Patriarchate, the Romanian Orthodox Church, Bucharest.

Hebrews 13:14 says, "For here we have no lasting city, but we seek the city which is to come." This Scripture reminds us of our theological task. We Christians are like strangers in a foreign country, with a faith that needs to be future-oriented, dynamic and relational.

Every theology, by its very nature, is unfinished business. It is a theology for pilgrims, a theology for one who is on the march. It is a process, always pointing to, rather than possessing, the truth. Thus, for this presentation, we are talking about *a* trinitarian theology, not *the* Trinitarian theology. Theology is faith seeking understanding for a specific context. It cannot be unthinkingly imposed from another context.

First comes doxology; then comes theology. Therefore, the theological task is both impossible and necessary. It is impossible in that we can never fully comprehend God. It is necessary because we have to talk about God if we are to talk meaningfully about humanity.

When we speak of theology, we must speak of three ways by which God works among us. We must speak of *koinonia* or theology as commitment to the community of faith, because distortion of truth rends apart the community. We speak of theology as *diakonia* or theology as service and self-giving; we recognize theology as *kerygma* or theology as proclamation or the mediation of religion to culture. In *koinonia*, one speaks the language of communion, in *diakonia* the language of contemplation and in *kerygma* the language of prophecy. The *shalom* of God's kingdom means freedom from sin, freedom from misery and freedom from despair in order to be free for love, justice and communion.

How can one judge whether good theologizing is being done? Good theology will have two marks about it: identity and relevance. In having identity, it will display continuity between its theologizing and the faith of the apostles. In having relevance, it will be intelligible and meaningful for its publics, shaping both their ethical framework and their actions.

A theologian, therefore, is both a child of one's time and, primarily, a person of faith. As a child of one's time, the theologian shifts with the shifting paradigms of the day. As a person of faith, the theologian lives out trust, taking God at God's word; belief, a commitment to the understanding of the creeds for today; and surrender.

Thus, theology is the work of the whole person to *kneel*, to *sit* and to *walk*. The theologian "kneels" before the mystery of God, not fully comprehending what one has experienced. It is said that we always know more than we understand and can understand more than we say. The theologian "sits"–does research and discusses with others the mystery of God so that thinking is done by the individual in community. Finally, the theologian "walks," because theological reflection is not simply written and proclaimed, but needs to be danced and sung. To truly be theology, it must satisfy the mind but must also be celebrated.

The city is now the most important context for doing theology. The city is most strategic in the plan of God today, because it is the city that is at the very vanguard of what God is doing in the world. Theology must therefore be done in the city and out of the experience of ministry if it is to effectively reflect God's plan for humanity. The future of the city determines the future of the world and therefore determines the future of theology.

The dominant paradigm for being able to do theology in the city must be *wonder and pain*—wonder at the city's technology but pain at how people are hurting and crushed by the systems driving that technology. Westerners tend to think disjunctively—that is, seeing everything in life as yes or no, as either-or. Asians and other Two-Thirds World people, however, think conjunctively, in this case including both wonder and pain. Thus, a human being, viewed from the West, was always seen as an individual substance having a rational nature. But this is a most inadequate understanding of humanity. Conjunctive thinking emphasizes that it is not only our intellect but our relationships that make us who we are, for we are nothing outside our relationships.

The theological task and the task of ministry must always go together. The doctrine of the Trinity provides for me the theological paradigm by which I understand my ministry. My ministry as priest to the garbage-dump scavengers of Smokey Mountain in Manila provides the context, the relationships and the community in which I think through and live out my trinitarian faith.

A major theme of the prophetic tradition of Israel is the conviction that real belief in God entails solidarity with the poor to ease their undeserved suffering by establishing *sedaqah* (justice) and *mishpat* (judgment). The God of Abraham, Isaac and Jacob wants justice to roll like a river (Amos 5:24). To go to the God of Jesus the Christ is to go to him in justice (Matt. 25:45). Love and justice cannot be separated for interpersonal relationships to be human and not become violent. This is all rooted in the conviction that God speaks to us through the signs of the times and events in history and calls us to build a society according to the principles of the kingdom.

The cries of the poor are signs of the times that reveal the divine plan operating in the redemptive love of Christ. The kingdom of God will change the present course of the world headed to destruction, eradicate all the demonic powers under which the world groans—ending all sorrow and pain, and bringing salvation for the people of God who are waiting for the fulfillment of the prophets' promises of a new world order where God will be all in all (1 Cor. 15:28).

How are we to speak of Father, Son and Holy Spirit in the midst of undeserved pain and suffering? Like Job who sat on a garbage heap (*mazbaleh,* Job 2:10), I also ask the same question. Like the Nazarene who cried out on Golgotha, which was the dumping ground for the refuse of Jerusalem, "My God, my God, why have you forsaken me?" (Matt. 27:45). We cannot properly understand the dramatic events of Golgotha except in terms of an explicit belief in the Trinity. Reality can be spoken of only in the language of the cross (1 Cor. 1:18-19) so that one can be committed without being a fanatic and be open-minded without being weak-willed in speaking of God from the standpoint of the poor, the deprived and the oppressed.

The passion, death and rising of Jesus was a trinitarian event, as Moltmann pointed out. The Father suffered the loss of his Son and his own fatherhood in the death of Jesus on the cross, thereby suffering the contradiction of great evil without angrily seeking revenge on his creatures who were responsible for his Son's death. The Son suffered the pain of death and of being forsaken by the Father. The Spirit reconciled the Father and Son in the very act of self-giving love and then communicated to human beings the trinitarian life, the power to overcome evil through self-giving love.

All creatures of the Father are immersed in the risen Christ and anointed by the Spirit to rediscover in the Scriptures the liberating aspect of the history of salvation and to discover that the struggle for liberation is prefigured in the Exodus and made real in the Paschal mystery. We discover, also, the fraternal living of the early Christian communities, which met in prayer and in the breaking of bread, sharing their goods and living united in heart and soul (Acts 2:42). These communities became instruments in the building of the kingdom of God, living sacraments of the salvific presence of God in the history of humanity. "We know that we have passed out of death into life, because we love the brethren" (1 John 3:14).

The crucified God, found among the weak and the oppressed and choosing to suffer with them, makes it possible to hope for a better tomorrow and to see the future as a communal adventure. In the resurrection of Jesus is grounded the Christian's radical openness to future possibilities. The crucified God, entering into the struggle for liberation in the person of Jesus, takes on the pain of human history in the Crucifixion and transforms it in the Resurrection. Thus, involvement to set prisoners free (Luke 4:18) constitutes a profound and spiritual experience where we have to encounter the real God.

Response by Ioan Sauca

Trinitarian theology from out of the Orthodox tradition has significant implications for city ministry. Witnessing to the Trinity is seen as very important both to Orthodox theology and its social understanding.

Witnessing to the Trinity gives the Orthodox Church a global understanding of God's work. It bases the life and work of the church in the Holy Trinity, not simply in its Christology. There is, consequently, an equal emphasis on all three persons of the Trinity in Orthodox theology, liturgy and praxis. Nothing in the world, to the Orthodox, is profane. All of life is sacred, created by God and blessed by the church. There is no separation of the transcendent and the imminent, eternity and time, faith and works, word and sacrament. All of life is one.

This global understanding overcomes the tension between the individual and the corporate, so that the person is understood only within the context of being a relational entity—the human person within the world, the Christian within the ecclesia. We are, therefore, strongly committed to the balance between the individual and the corporate in all arenas of life.

This balance was modeled in Basil the Great and in the Cappadocians, who established the town named Basilciudade to care for the needy (including an orphanage and a hospital for Christians, Jews and pagans). This town existed as a living example of how ministry emerged from a Trinitarian-based theology and faith.

The Impact of
Feminist Theology on Urban Mission

From a presentation by Dorothy McRae-McMahon, director of the Commission for Mission of the Uniting Church in Australia and a clergyperson of the Uniting Church. Rev. McRae-McMahon lives in Sydney, Australia.

When we minister in an urban context, what we do tells people who we think God is. It is upon that realization that one can most clearly appreciate the contribution feminist theology makes to urban ministry.

Feminist theology asks all of us to step out into our own personal experience and name our own pain and celebration. This means that one must question a patriarchal or authoritarian way of looking at life. Through feminist theology women are asked to lead as well as to follow, to be free to be weak or strong, and to be open to the pain and gifts of all people.

In an urban context where there is so much systemic oppression, the tendency will be for women to simply engage in the struggles of those with whom we minister and who are marginalized or exploited by these systems. This is an essential task of urban ministry. But it must not ignore our own oppression as women. We must recognize oppressions within oppressions and thus recognize that we as women have our own interior work to do and our own feminist oppression, as well as the exploitation felt by the poor, powerless and marginalized.

Even the theology we articulate as a church may contribute to the oppression of women—not intentionally, but simply because it comes unconsciously out of a paternalistic paradigm. Feminist spiritually teaches us that to connect with our vulnerability is both acceptable and healthy. Therefore, the very nature of spirituality demands pain and joy. Anger and hurt must sometimes stand rather than be resolved. Perceiving God as one who carries the wholeness of our femaleness and maleness richly adds to our liturgy. So often, traditional theology informs but does not engage one in the struggles of life because it is only cerebral in nature. But life is much more than the act of thinking.

How do people change? Westerners think that people change by giving them additional information. Most of our education and even the communication of ethical standards is based on the premise that if people know more about a subject, they will choose the good or the wise course. But that is not what truly changes us. What changes us is to be in a safe enough context where we are encouraged to both act and reflect, to weep and to be angry. Information can be used to help resource me as I am in the process of changing, but it will not bring about my transformation. People must act to liberate themselves.

In the paradigm of the Cross, God asks us to enter pain and death—and yet, there is resurrection on the other side. The word "compassion" in Hebrew literally means "womb space." When someone shares with me about the poor, for example, I worry about what will be asked of me; I feel guilty, angry, intimidated. But if I accept and live into my pain, God has the opportunity to work in me and free me so that I can commit myself to those who frighten me—but do so with trembling. It is only when we pretend to be powerful or strong that we are weak. It is when we admit to ourselves our vulnerability and live into it that God can reveal God's call to us. Feminist theology, therefore, is power *for*, not power *over*—a profoundly different way of understanding power.

What feminist theology can most contribute to the urban church is the need to have answers. To truly be the church in the city is to be community, to create space that just lets people work together on their respective pain. It is working together as a community, not as a hierarchy.

Our courage to be honest with ourselves and with each other creates the conditions in which authentic community can be built. Only the creation of authentic community in a specific time and place and with a specific people will truly recreate the church. Only when community is created can the church effectively undertake its business of being the church with the poor, the marginalized and the hurting of the city.

Remnant Theology as the Base for Urban Ministry

From a presentation by John Vincent, director of the Urban Theology Unit, Sheffield and a clergyperson of the Methodist Church in Great Britain. Dr. Vincent lives in Sheffield, England. A response is given by Carol Ann McGibbon, vice president of the Seminary Consortium for Urban Pastoral Education, Chicago.

Theology takes place as the people of God see themselves as part of the biblical story, project themselves into that story and then project that story out into their corporate and individual lives. It arises from disciples of Jesus Christ looking in a mirror to discern who they are as Christians.

All theology is a variety of paradigms with which one interacts and reflects as a Christian while part of the gospel unfolds. It is the end point in a process—a personal discipline, arising from a particular person at a particular time and in a particular context seeking to address a particular issue of the church, the world or the Christian life.

Within that understanding of the theological task, how does the urban situation inform biblical reflection? Which paradigms in the biblical stories make sense for ministry in the urban context? I believe that the tradition of the remnant provides the most hope for the urban church.

The biblical paradigm of the remnant is that of a people who vicariously commit themselves to the world, are willing to suffer in seeking its redemption and thereby embody in their life together a new society. This vicarious vocation of the few reaches its apex in the figure of Christ. It makes the most sense for the calling of the church in the city but as always, it will be in conflict with the church as chaplaincy.

There is much that is lost by doing ministry from a remnant theology. Maintaining and building the church as an institution can no longer be an end of the church. Understanding self-worth by building a great congregation or by administering a successful enterprise becomes totally inappropriate.

But this approach does mean a church that takes seriously the saviorship both of Christ and of the church, the faithful few within an alien world. It means the embodiment of a new society lived out before the world, both confronting and being confronted by the values of the society of the day. It means the willingness to be small, weak and rejected—but always in the light of final victory in the consummation. It means that the church see itself as God intends it to be in our urban context.

Some questions must be asked, however. Does embracing remnant theology offer any real hope for having a significant effect upon society? Is such discipleship of any use, or is it simply throwing one's life away? Would not a world-affirming model that supports and is affirmed by the city's "principalities and powers" be more effective? These are the questions that would tempt us.

The reality is that our expectations under the discipline of a remnant theology undergo significant change. The church becomes an advocate of another society, the kingdom of God. The church becomes more "feminine"— more tending, nurturing and caring. The church becomes in its life and ministry a vicarious redeemer, continuing the ongoing work of God in the world through God's servant remnant. The church becomes a survivor at, and along with, the bottom of society rather than the triumphalistic, established body of the status quo.

This is the call of faith and faithfulness that is today coming to the urban church as it seeks to identify with the suffering, the marginalized and the "little ones" of the city.

Response by Carol Ann McGibbon:

The essential question is "To whom does theology belong? Who is the creator and forger of theology?" For too long, the theological task has been in the hands of the powerful, the elite and the academic.

The task of those who undertake ministry in the city is to work with the poor so that areas clouded by confusion give way to clear thinking. It is not the task of the church in the city to form a new elitism, but rather to identify with the marginalized of society and to theologize in that context. Whatever we put together theologically, we must be able to take back to our situation.

When reflecting on the paradigm of remnant theology, we need to do so from the perspective of a theology of hope that is rooted in Christ's story and the story of the Old Testament people. This is a theology of survival that brings people close to God and to one other. Vision must be the prophetic element of remnant theology–seeing through the given to the reality of the kingdom of God in the city, as God would have reality to be.

A Theology of Urban Mission:
An Orthodox Perspective

From a presentation by Ioan Sauca, a priest of the Romanian Orthodox Church and executive secretary for Orthodox Studies and Relationships in Mission, Unit II, the World Council of Churches. Fr. Sauca lives in Geneva, Switzerland. A response is given by Dorothy McRae-McMahon, director of the Commission for Mission of the Uniting Church in Australia.

Why are there differences in the practice and principles of missiology? Differences in missiology occur because of differences in ecclesiology. Mission is an expression of the church's theology. Mission and theology are often thought of as two distinct disciplines but are actually inseparable. Mission cannot be separated from the church's life and belief; it is an inextricable part of the church's very being. The Orthodox church states that the church's ecclesiology in itself is missionary, based upon Acts 1:8: "And you shall be my witnesses."

The word "mission" is used to define the actions of the church. Just as the church and mission are inseparable, so the theology of one implies the theology of the other. Today, mission often becomes a separate institution. As a result, mission begins to operate alongside of the church instead of being an integral part of the church. Perspective becomes lost; it is forgotten that mission is part of the very being of the church.

An Orthodox perspective on a theology of urban mission begins with the recognition that the church has been given the very gifts it needs to carry out the fulfillment of the kingdom of God. This becomes the mission focus of the church: to lead the whole world to this kingdom. The church can then be used as a laboratory of our resurrection into the new creation as Christ is being actualized in us.

There are three major implications of this type of theology. First, the church's mission is Christ's mission. It is the sign of the kingdom of God's re-creation of the world. Second, the source of mission then becomes the church. The goal is for the church to exemplify itself as a sacramental community, a symbol of the kingdom. Third, the city is the dwelling place of the church. Christ's body is actualized in the sacramental presence of the church in the community.

In Orthodox ecclesiology, the relationship between the local church and the community is vitally important. Instead of ordaining priests for the people as a whole, priests are ordained for specific communities. "A person sanctifies the place" and thus is "sanctified to God in the community." In Orthodox theology, every nation, city and family has a patron angel. The city becomes a blessing because it is God's creation. To transform the city, then, one must begin by transforming people's lives.

Three common values emerge from the insight that Christ is present in the city in the sacramental presence of the church. First, the church must share the *kerygma*, being God's presence in the city and proclaiming it. A worshiping, praying presence is most important of all. Christian mission can be lived out only through the community of faith committed to the worship of God.

Second, liturgy is not confined to the church but is the life of the Orthodox Christian. Liturgy continues into the week in daily prayers and Christian witness. It is an act carried out daily in life and work. Third, the liturgy of the church during the week must be incarnated by sharing in the suffering of the poor and the weak. This service comes out of the spiritual depths of the people of God.

Several barriers exist for the mission of the church in the city. People in today's cities are losing touch with God and God's kingdom by finding no permanent place in which to dwell. Instead of anchoring in one specific church, people move from one church to another, having no real sense of belonging. The priests no longer know the people. Stemming from this lack of community, laity and priests become afraid of reaching out to nonbelievers because a fear exists that they may not have the "right answers." People forget that we witness, but God converts.

The church in the city must also deal with the seduction of materialism and secularism. Conversion comes through the prayers of a community and honest confessions and sharing of the faith. The urban church must also grapple with the lack of cooperation in doing missions.

Orthodox ecclesiology insists that mission and the church are one and inseparable. The church is there to reach out to the people of the community, yet this is becoming increasingly more difficult to accomplish amid the current situation in our cities. However, there are several ways for missions to cooperate and multiply their efforts. Possibilities include holding joint activities, exchanging missionary experiences and working together on common social issues.

Response by Dorothy McRae-McMahon

There are three important gifts the Orthodox tradition gives to the whole body of Christ. The first gift is the insight that mission is essential to the very being of the church. The church needs to be expressing this being in the rhythm of worship by developing a true community that comes before the Lord in praise and thanksgiving.

The second gift of the Orthodox tradition is the fact that mission must be seen in an eschatological context. This keeps us both from burnout and missionary arrogance. It also prevents despair from developing as we are forced to look at our work from the big picture.

The third gift is that mission is sacramental. This occurs as the Crucifixion and Resurrection become patterns in life. For the poor, this is particularly relevant as they can understand this out of their own experiences and out of the sacrament.

History and Context

The Challenge of Today's Urban World

From a presentation by Jimmy Maroney, an urban and research specialist on the staff of the Foreign Mission Board of the Southern Baptist Convention (USA). He makes his home in Richmond, USA.

Humankind has been on this globe for a minimum of one million years. Cities have existed only during the last 7,000 years. With respect to social, economic and cultural dominance, the city as a dominant player has been much shorter. Cities have been islands in a rural sea. Two hundred years ago, the world was 97 percent rural. Ninety-one years ago the world was six-sevenths rural.

Such is not the case today. The cities have become central to the future of the world. They dominate the economic life, political decision-making, communications, entertainment and social fabric not only of their countries, but of their regions and the world as well. At the same time as its rise to dominance, the growth and power of cities has gravitated toward the Two-Thirds World. In 1950, 23 of the 35 world's largest agglomerations were located in the developed world. By 1985, however, the distribution had completely reversed itself with 23 of the 35 largest urban agglomerations situated in the less developed world. United Nations projections (1990) suggest that by 2005, 17 of the 20 largest cities will be in the developing nations.

We see the dominance by cities of their nations and regions in the examples of Tokyo and Seoul. In the richest nation in the world, the city of Tokyo dominates the economic, cultural and academic life of the nation. Sixty percent of Japan's top business leaders live in Tokyo, 60 percent of Japan's total invested capital is there, 33.3 percent of deposited banking accounts, 33.3 percent of university graduates, 21 percent of tertiary industry income,

27 percent of retail and wholesale sales, 15 percent of sale of manufactured products, 15 percent of Japan's working population in secondary industry, 33.3 percent of department store sales, 25 percent of entertainment admissions, 20 percent of Japan's universities, 50 percent of university students, 60 percent of heads of industrial and commercial enterprises all center in Tokyo (source: Tokyo Metropolitan Government, 1984).

Seoul likewise dominates Korea. Seventy-eight percent of the headquarters of business firms and 90 percent of large business enterprises are housed there. Seoul accounts for 28 percent of the nation's value added by manufacturing, 25 percent of the nation's total manufacturing employment, 32.3 percent of all manufacturing establishments, 65 percent of all loans and deposits, 55 percent of all colleges and universities, 50 percent of all medical doctors and specialists, 50 percent of the national wealth, and 27.9 percent of South Korea's 1977 GNP (source: Cong-Won Chu, "Issues on Housing," 1980).

Historically, cities were created by planned intent, shaped by their respective national governments for specific purposes, derived their power from their government, and had a vested interest in maintaining the status quo. The modern city, on the other hand, is created by default (no one plans it), it is shaped by market forces, its power is based on its performance (particularly in the economic sector) and its vested interest lies in continuing and escalating change.

A look at four major cities provides for us a synopsis of both the issues and the potentials facing the church for urban ministry.

Journalists throughout the world frequently cite Calcutta as a clear example of urban pathology—of what the future may hold for other cities in developing countries that fail to control rapid urban growth. Numerous articles have discussed the scores of thousands of pavement dwellers on the Calcutta streets, the visible evidence of widespread unemployment and absolute poverty, and the severe congestion and infrastructure collapse.

More than two-thirds of Calcutta's population have monthly incomes of less than the equivalent of US$35; at least 1.5 million persons are unemployed. More than one-third of the city's inhabitants live in 3,000 unregistered slums or squatter settlements. The city's water supply system and sewerage network was constructed by the colonial government in the nineteenth century; it is now inadequate and obsolete, and severe drainage problems make much of the city impassable during the monsoon season. Because of its limited road space (the last major road inside the city was built half a century ago) and the large number of slow-moving vehicles, the traffic problems of Calcutta are among India's worst. All these problems are made more acute by the city's very high population densities (more than 1,235 persons per hectare in certain central wards) and by its very low income levels, which make cost recovery very difficult (source: The Metropolis Era, Dogan/Kasarda).

New York City is a threatened city. The forces of external competition now appear to pose a major threat to New York's economic leadership of the world. Financial markets in London and Tokyo have expanded rapidly since their recent deregulation, and Tokyo has benefited from the amassed surpluses of Japan's export trade, which have made Japan's banks dominant in the world since the mid-1980s. The office sectors in London and Tokyo are undergoing major expansion, thus providing the increased volumes of more competitively priced space in which to house their expanding finance and service industries. From all evidence, New York-based corporations in both the financial and the advanced business services industries will also participate in the wave of expansion in London and Tokyo, but the locus of new global activity could well occur outside New York City.

New competitive financial centers are also appearing in Hong Kong, in Singapore, and within the United States in Los Angeles. Further assaults on New York's concentration of activities come from the spinning out of back office and middle-market activities to its suburban neighbors; in addition, the services and finance industries have expanded in rapidly growing regional centers in Atlanta, Boston, Seattle, Dallas and Miami (source: Cities in a Global Society).

Shanghai is packed as tightly as a matchbox. Up to 425,000 people squeeze into a square mile of Shanghai's inner city. Most homes have little space for anything but beds, with three generations often sleeping in a single room. What housing there is in Shanghai lacks the basic amenities taken for granted in other cities of the world. Too many people fight for too few goods in too little space, creating a nasty blend of pollution, poverty, over-crowding, shortages and corruption.

The average Shanghaiese lives without toilet or bathing facilities in a room about the size of a double bed. He nestles with his wife in park bushes on summer nights for lack of privacy at home, bringing along his marriage license to show inquiring police. He breathes air that is polluted 10 times worse than American standards allow. He drinks water that is mainly chlorinated sewage and eats vegetables laced with industrial toxins, factors contributing to stomach cancer. He fights with three others for every available space on the bus. Raw sewage leaks into the streets of Shanghai's older sections, overflowing septic tanks. Housewives walk a block or more to draw water from public standpipes, lugging heavy buckets or balancing them on bamboo poles. They cook on primi-

tive coal stoves in communal kitchens or in outdoor cor-
ridors clouded in coal dust. As a center for huge oil
refineries and chemical and metallurgical plants, Shanghai is also the home of the "Yellow Dragons"–local slang
for the sulphurous clouds that pour out of the factory
chimneys (source: Dogan/Kasarda).

Tokyo is now approaching the threshold of the
world's first 30 million population supercity. With economic, political and cultural institutions juxtaposed and
mingled together, Tokyo offers a wide variety of opportunities. Unemployment and crime rates are minimal, and
very few people talk about Tokyo's problems. But the
housing situation is notorious, and is not being dealt with
in the revolutionary way it requires. While admitting that
"rabbit hutches" inhabited by the affluent are the result of
poor policy, small houses are seen as being handy for
those too lazy or too busy to clean or organize larger
places.

The majority of Tokyo citizens are apparently satis-
fied. The media reports all sorts of urban problems
throughout the world–internal strife, robberies, kidnap-
pings, vandalism, racial segregation, fires, social and economic discrepancies, and on and on. Many believe that
Tokyo will remain unaffected by these problems. There is
an economic imbalance in Tokyo between rich and poor,
but most are more or less content with their present situation. Most consider themselves to be middle class and
able to consider making a trip abroad, which until
recently was out of reach for most people. There has been
a rapid influx of foreigners, some coming legitimately as
teachers, technicians, merchants, lawyers or students, but
many coming illegally as cheap labor.

As these four scenarios illustrate, there are primary
forces at work in the growth of giant cities. They tend to
be ninefold (source: Dogan/Kasarda).

❖ High rates of unemployment and underemploy-
ment as urban labor markets are unable to absorb
the expanding numbers of urban job seekers
❖ Insufficient housing and shelter
❖ Health and nutrition problems
❖ Inadequate sanitation and water supplies
❖ Overloaded and congested transportation sys-
tems
❖ Air, water and noise pollution
❖ Municipal budget crises
❖ Rising crime and other social malaise
❖ A general deterioration of the perceived quality
of urban life

We will here look at four essential urban problems.

Migration

Migration is one of the two primary factors leading
to the rapid growth of the world's cities (the other is
birthrate). In most Two-Thirds World cities, immigration
contributes to about half of the growth in city population
in any year. It is, therefore, a major contributor both to
the incapacity of the city to provide adequate services
and to the growth in urban poverty.

I must make two points regarding urban migrants.
First, we must not assume that all migrants are poverty-
stricken and living in a generally deprived state. Some
migrants probably have at least as much access to income
and services as nonmigrants. Moreover, there are advan-
tages in the urban area that, in the mind of the migrant,
at least help to compensate for the city's disadvantages.
Thus, although not all aspects of city life are favorable, we
must not conclude that migration automatically makes
people worse off than they were in the village or on the
farm.

Second, many of the migrants' problems tend to be common to both men and women or to a family unit. Thus, it would be misleading to discuss them only in relation to a certain category of migrants. This reservation is important because it would be wrong to consider a number of special problems just for women (for example) in cases where the need is much broader.

Urban communications

As the great world cities have become more closely bonded together into a global society, they have also been pulled away from their national hinterlands. What some see as a global network of cities, others see as a global network of corporations creating channels through which business is conducted. The problem is that while the world economy becomes more integrated, the sociopolitical structure of individual world cities becomes more segmented, leading to loss of cohesion and community within cities. The whole city is not linked to the global economy; only selected groups within a city may be accentuated if some groups are more fully linked to the global economy than others.

Despite efforts to preserve nationalism and traditionalism, few towns in the world are truly isolated. Telecommunication, television, audiotapes, VCRs, satellite broadcasts and cable television have greatly increased communication. Yucatan housewives watch soap operas in small one-room thatched-roof huts of a style 1,000 years old. Television antennas appear in squatters' houses on the hills of Rio de Janeiro or in the outskirts of Lima. This, and increased international travel, has brought more awareness and rising expectations. Ideas travel fast; even international terrorists have learned to exploit the media.

Urban ecological problems

New issues have come up in city planning and city development pointing to a general responsibility that the city bears beyond its own limits. The dying forests of Europe, for instance, and other urgent ecological warnings all over the world point out the need to reduce air pollution drastically. Studies about air pollution created by traffic, however, clearly tell us that technical means alone will not suffice. How can the functions in a city region be allocated in a way that reduces traffic? The cities in Switzerland, for example, are now looking for ways to cut down automobile traffic by about 30 percent.

Other sources of ecological problems are agricultural and industrial, depending on how they produce, which materials they use and what kind of technology they employ. Disposal of garbage has become a top ecological issue—especially highly toxic garbage. Even tourism becomes a problem: the more beautiful a place is, the more likely it is that visitors will destroy it.

Poverty and powerlessness

Both the number and percentage of the poor found in the world's cities is overwhelming and is growing steadily. The church, in particular, cannot ignore both the presence and the plight of the urban poor.

There are the economic consequences of urban poverty: unemployment and underemployment, low income, limited education, inadequate diet, lack of breast-feeding, the growth in prostitution and other means of illegally generating income. There are the environmental implications of urban poverty: inadequate water and sanitation, over-crowding, poor or no housing, lack of land to grow food, lack of rubbish disposal, traffic, hazardous waste disposal, infectious diseases, pollution, accidents, consumption of junk foods. There are the psychosocial distresses of urban poverty: stress, alienation, instability, insecurity, depression, substance abuse and abandoned children.

Underlying the poverty of a city and the marginalization and victimization of its poor is the entire way urban power is exercised. Power in a city grows quietly, and information on it and its outreach is not easily discovered. That power is manifested in two ways. There is the political and economic, largely depersonalized processes of power, resulting in the manipulation, exploitation and oppression of whole categories of urban people. Second, behind the depersonalized processes of power lie individuals and groups that play a key role in these political processes, maintaining or promoting them, sometimes unwittingly. Access to power is often obscure in large organizations, and it can happen that some practically unknown person who occupies a strategic position in an urban bureaucracy has more power than the person at the pinnacle of the official political pyramid.

In order for the church to adequately affect the city and make an impact on the problems there, missionaries and ministers must be able to not only identify the problems but to locate their source. This includes identifying those people who have the political, economic and value-setting powers within the city that can bring about change. We are not fighting faceless enemies, but we must identify who or what is behind each problem. If missionaries continue to assume that the power structure is some great, unidentifiable force it becomes difficult to provoke change. Instead, to make a difference, it becomes necessary to both understand urban policies and locate power.

Historical Reflections
on Urban Ministry in America

From a presentation by Clifford Green, professor of Theology at Hartford Seminary, Hartford, Connecticut, USA, and editor of a study of urban ministry in the United States between 1945 and 1985.

The issue for urban ministry is not the "inner city" or the "urban poor" seen in an objectified way from some secure suburban isolation. Rather, looking at urban metropolitan areas as a whole, we must see the problem as one of disparity and contradiction between rich and poor, suburb and city, Anglo-Americans and people of color. In this light, urban areas are microcosms of national and global disparities. This is the inescapable context of ministry challenging the whole church today.

Since all ministry and theology is contextual, we have to preach the gospel and be the church in ways that address this context. We dare not speak of evangelism, salvation, new life, repentance and reconciliation, community with God and with one another, the love of Christ, the Christian life of faith, hope and love, apart from this context. The work of the Holy Spirit must be related to this public social world, not confined to individualistic and subjective (spiritual!) interpretations. The church must proclaim and live out the gospel of reconciliation and liberation in relation to this social reality.

The study by ten American denominations of their churches' urban strategies was informed by several questions. What has the central concept of "urban ministry" meant, and what forms has it taken? What paradigm of the city has informed the urban ministry of churches? How have racism and urban poverty been addressed? What role have the laity had in urban ministry? Have ecumenical strategies been important? What has been the relationship of urban and suburban congregations?

Two great migrations have shaped urban society in North America during this century. The first is the migration of African Americans from the rural south to northern industrial cities, accompanied by a northerly Hispanic migration. The second was "white flight," as more affluent Anglo-Americans created suburbs and moved to them after World War II. A great deal of church resources went into "new church development" as suburbs burgeoned. But as the city-suburb split grew, leaders of urban ministry began a counter-cultural movement to relate the gospel to changing urban life, especially problems of racism, poverty and the breakdown of urban community.

In the 1960s, especially under the leadership of Dr. Martin Luther King, Jr., a great deal of urban ministry focused on civil rights, with marches and demonstrations, anti-racism workshops and advocacy for legislation. During this period, established black urban congregations received new members from the southern migration, which also gave rise to new congregations, frequently taking over sanctuaries left by white flight to the suburbs. These churches had a special ministry, namely to protect, affirm and nurture the people of God who were oppressed by a racist society. The pastors of these churches often played important public roles, e.g., serving on city councils and boards of education, as leaders in election campaigns, in organizations like the National Association for the Advancement of Colored People (NAACP) and the Urban League, and testifying before government bodies. Much more than their white counterparts, black churches frequently served as meeting places for social and political groups, and did a better job of holding together the gospel and the issues of urban community and social justice.

A dramatic phenomenon of the period beginning about 1961 was the rise of church-based urban training or action training centers. Supported by 15 national church agencies, 27 centers were set up in 22 cities, and hundreds of clergy who worked in cities across the country gained conceptual and practical tools for their ministry in urban areas.

Perhaps the most enduring development was the rise of community organizing as a widespread strategy for addressing urban ills. Inspired by Saul Alinsky's methods, organizing was essentially a strategy of politically empowering communities to solve their own problems. In the first stage, congregations were often recruited to support the efforts of coalitions of community groups. In the more recent second stage, however, church-based community organizing has developed as coalitions of neighborhood churches have taken their own neighborhood initiatives, often transforming the congregation in the process. By reflecting on the context of this urban ministry history, we can see two broad groupings in church strategies during this period—those that are congregation-based and those that are based in structures of coalitions with a metropolitan focus. Another observation from the history is that urban ministry in the United States has tended to focus on a series of issues, as is characteristic of the culture as a whole: civil rights, poverty, public housing, hunger, homelessness and so on. By itself, a focus on issues cannot raise basic systemic issues about the nature of a city as such, its morphology, structure and dynamics, and what this might imply for churches' urban strategies.

What are the implications of viewing the city as a whole, a metropolis of interdependent parts? First, this means not adopting the fractured model of city and suburbs that defines urban ministry as concerned with the "inner city." Suburban congregations must be as concerned about the "peace of the city" (Jer. 29:5ff) as are those in the core city.

Second, the critical issues just mentioned are seen in a new framework. Since these issues are no respecters of denominations, an ecumenical strategy, pursued through metropolitan ecumenical forms, is necessary (whether local councils of churches will serve this purpose is an open question).

Third, we need new thinking and forms of action about the role of the laity in urban-metropolitan mission. This must be particularly seen in their vocational settings and public responsibilities. Lay people, in large numbers, are a scattered, uncoordinated diaspora throughout the institutions of the city: government, industry, education, law, business, finance, medicine, the media—all the institutions that bear on the life and crises of modern cities. We need forms of the church, parallel to the congregation, to support lay ministry in public life through: (1) common study of the Bible, theology and ethics, and (2) cooperative reflection to clarify policies and plan strategies for their work institutions and public roles.

I am convinced that the components of a comprehensive urban-metropolitan ministry strategy need to be as follows:

❖ Urban ministry needs to be based on an understanding and analysis of the metropolis as a whole, not dividing churches between "inner city" and "suburban," which reflects the class and race structure of society.

❖ Urban and suburban congregations would be linked, both in particular relationships, and in a metropolitan ecumenical council of churches.

❖ The metropolitan ecumenical council would be the vehicle for local denominational agencies (judicatories) to pursue a common urban strategy.

❖ Urban congregations, in cooperation with others in their neighborhoods, would be sponsors and participants in community organizing for their neighborhoods.

❖ Laity in their work roles and institutions would be regarded as prime bearers of the church's urban ministry; members of different congregations and denominations would be ecumenically linked for training and mutual support.

❖ The churches' practice of urban ministry would be thoroughly ecumenical as this involves cooperation between congregations, judicatories and laity.

❖ The church would be committed to addressing systemic causes of urban ills and injustices through multiple strategies of advocacy, social investment and community organizing, and not only responding to crises and emergency needs.

❖ Urban ministry would be informed by a public theology that understands the gospel and the Bible to be as pertinent to social, economic and political life as it is to individuals and personal relationships.

The History of the
City Missions Movement

From a presentation by Michael Eastman, secretary (director) of the Frontier Youth Trust, a ministry among urban alienated youth that is associated with Scripture Union. He is a Baptist from London, United Kingdom.

In the late 1800s and the early 1900s, cities in Great Britain began to go through a process of industrialization. This industrialization resulted in unprecedented growth in the cities, causing a more noticeable gap between the rich people already situated in the city and the poor people coming into it for employment. Close to the same time, a religious awakening was occurring throughout the English-speaking world.

As a result, people began to take more seriously the needs of those hurting around them. This included a heightened awareness of the needs of the city and its people. This combination of growth within the cities, industrialization and a movement of religious awakening resulted in the mid-nineteenth century in the emergence of voluntary societies promoting social change while promoting the spread of the gospel. This commitment to social change resulted in a ministry that was able to serve both the physical and spiritual needs of the poor within the city. As these voluntary societies began to develop and grow in capacity, they began to raise money to send their own people on overseas missions.

People such as David Naismith (1799-1879) and Jerry McAuley were instrumental in the creation and development of the city missions movement. This was integral to the effort that created voluntary mission societies throughout the world. Naismith and McAuley began voluntary societies that raised money to support people from their very own neighborhood in reaching out to the surrounding community and bring its members to faith. A compassion developed toward the poor and their needs, resulting in a recognition of the need to invest personal interest, fortune and effort in the cities. Naismith and McAuley did this by helping to form a society, which in turn visited within each urban district, organized to address social need and brought the poor to Christ, mobilizing them to deal with their own social issues. In this manner every soul was seen as being of inestimable worth. Everyone counted.

City missions have historically been characterized by their personal approach. The movement began as individuals within the community began to make personal contact with one another. Individuals, families, women and children were all an integral part of the city missions movement within the neighborhoods. Without their participation, it would never have evolved as it did. This made the city missions movement lay centered. Women were valued very highly in this movement and as a result it became very liberating for them. The movement was characterized by a hands-on approach. You did not talk about, you went and did it; you walked it, you knew it. City missions focused on understanding people and the unique groups of which they were a part.

The city missions movement focused on specific people groups within the community. This could include cabbies, construction workers, businessmen and so on. Most of the workers involved in the movement did not receive any formal training or education regarding their work. Instead, they "learned by doing." While they were learning, the city's mission movement began to grow rapidly. As it grew, social care agencies were formed that served to fulfill the needs of the urban poor. These social care programs focused on food distribution, health care, confronting sexual exploitation and other important social issues.

City missions were interdenominational in nature, making them unique at their time of development. As opposed to focusing on church affiliation, city missions movements were able to focus more on the plethora of human need that needed addressing. The primary objective of the city's missions movement was to convert the whole social class of the urban poor to Christianity. Because of the propensity and size of the movement, a "professional" missionary team was unable to reach everyone. Therefore, a large ecumenical, lay leadership developed that was both practical and task-centered.

An important outcome of the city missions movement was the expectation that every Christian would be involved in social issues. This marked a radical change and development from previous eras. As a consequence of this large lay involvement and the perception that every Christian should be involved with social issues and missions, Christian values were diffused throughout the city. An important impact of this movement was the establishment of what would be the root and foundations of the 20th Century Welfare Station in Britain. Together with other social and political movements, this resulted in the betterment of an entire social class. As a result new churches were created that focused on the importance of lay leadership. As a social conscience was awakened in existing churches, this led to increasing involvement in social concern, social care and social justice.

Today, the city missions movement focuses on resurgency, renewal, reappraisal (learning from the cities and the past), networking and the development of new movements. Unlike the early movement, the emphasis today is placed on examining the roots of urban poverty and focusing on prevention as well as practical care. Instead of entering the city as an individual, the missions movement focuses on the community, looking to individuals within the area to develop into leaders and thus work to make changes. No longer are missionaries considered the rescuers; instead, they are considered agents of social change, facilitating movements from within the community and neighborhoods. A continuity remains as twelve of the early agencies are still in operation today. New missions are still being created resulting in a resurgence of the movement. A renewal is happening with young people being particularly involved with "hands-on" types of opportunities. Finally, a reappraisal is occurring with new movements and changes taking place. We can learn much from the history of the city missions movement.

History of Urban Training Centers

From a presentation by Carol Ann McGibbon, vice president of the Seminary Consortium for Urban Pastoral Education (SCUPE), an urban training center in Chicago, USA. SCUPE provides the means for the preparation of seminarians for urban ministry from a wide spectrum of Chicago-based theological schools. Rev. McGibbon lives in Chicago, USA.

In this presentation, I wish to examine the development and decline of the urban training centers in North America, examining why, after 20 years, the very action centers that were developed to promote urban social change have met their demise within the United States. We will do this by examining two action training centers that have survived—one in Canada and the other in Puerto Rico.

Urban training occurred at a time when great social change was happening in the United States. Initially, 27 action centers were developed in 22 cities in New York, Chicago, Atlanta, Cleveland, Nashville, Washington and Seattle. The centers were ecumenical in nature. They received most of their funding from sources outside the local congregations, such as foundations. Twenty years after their development, however, most of the urban training centers are closed.

Why? I would suggest five contributing factors to the demise of the urban training center movement.

❖ Seminaries did not incorporate the movement into their curriculum.

❖ If supported by seminaries, there was no owner-
ship and therefore no funding. There was accred-
itation but no investment.

❖ There were controversies over how to do theological education in cities, particularly over a contextual approach versus a formal, academic
approach.

❖ A difficulty existed in sustaining denominational
funding.

❖ Confusion existed about how to use power in the
city—especially regarding community organizing.

All of the above issues are very real and still exist
today.

While the action training centers in the United
States have continued to die, that has not been the case
outside America. Two programs that have continued to
thrive are the Canadian Urban Training Project for Christian Service (CUTS) in Toronto, Canada and PRISA in
Puerto Rico.

The differences in approach and action between the
American centers and these efforts present an intriguing
contrast and possible guidelines for future training center
development. Much of their success is gleaned from the
goals of the two organizations. Unlike the early action
centers, CUTS and PRISA have committed themselves to:

❖ Keep the agenda of urban mission before the
whole church;

❖ Refocus the mission effort of the church to the
local urban context, rather than simply overseas;
and

❖ Target church planting in inner-city locations.

Each of these three goals has resulted in the sustaining of these programs, unlike the 27 once found in the

United States. Besides the goals of each institution, we can learn much from the purpose statements of both CUTS and PRISA.

The purpose of CUTS is to:

❖ Train and equip Christian clergy and laity to relate the work of the Christian church to the life of metropolitan areas.
❖ Establish courses of study and training programs to the end that clergy and laity may better understand the urban culture and interpret the Christian faith within such culture.
❖ Gather information concerning the life and problems of metropolitan areas, such as planning, urban renewal and slum clearance as this information relates to the work of the Christian church, and to make this information widely available.
❖ Evoke new forms and patterns for Christian service within existing church structures wherever possible.

Similarly, PRISA is loyal to the Christian faith, while maintaining a commitment to the political, economic, social and cultural change in its country. PRISA is also committed to working with diverse groups of people while promoting human liberation.

Both PRISA and CUTS have been able to survive where similar organizations have failed because of their ability to combine social action with the agenda and context of the church. Both programs also tried to adapt to their situations. They are both decentralized in nature, both in decision-making and programming. The two programs have managed to maintain a tension between their social responsibility and the institutionalized church.

Both are also highly ecumenical in nature. The combination of these factors has resulted in two sustainable organizations from which much can be learned regarding the sustainability of action training centers.

Urban Missiology

A New Way of Being Church

From a presentation by Benigno Beltran, whose credentials were presented earlier in this book. Fr. Beltran discussed his personal experience of his work among the people of Smokey Mountain in Manila, the Philippines. "A new way of being church" is an example of what Beltran called "bearing witness to the suffering Christ among the poorest of the poor."

The vision upon which we have built our ministry in Smokey Mountain is a vision of a Trinitarian ministry. Journeying to the Father (the God-before-us) in the company of the Son (the God-with-us) and under the guidance of the Holy Spirit (the God-within-us), the people of God in the Parish of the Risen Christ in Smokey Mountain join hands in building up the kingdom of truth, peace and justice according to the gospel in solidarity with the poorest of the poor.

Smokey Mountain is the name of a squatter settlement located on a garbage dump in Manila. The community has approximately 3,019 families, with a population of 18,000 to 20,000 people. The average family has six children. Many visitors to the site make the automatic assumption that most of the people in the community would move if they had the chance. This is not true, however, as Smokey Mountain has formed a close-knit community. This intense commitment to each other was demonstrated by the fact that even though the government had once evacuated the community, a majority returned. There are three explanations for this phenomenon:

- ❖ A sense of community keeps them there;
- ❖ A sentimental attachment to the land; and
- ❖ Relative ease of finding odd jobs within the vicinity.

This tight community is not something that is visibly apparent, but through time and throughout history has proven true.

On January 17, 1992, President Aquino signed Memorandum 415, which would create habitable housing on the dump site for the residents. The president had good intentions but failed to recognize or understand the complete situation. By constructing homes on top of the dump site, the government would be taking away the community's livelihood, since the income of 70 percent of the residents in the area is derived from sorting the garbage and selling it for recycling.

Poverty as lived by Christ demands of us solidarity with the poor, the oppressed and marginal groups living on the periphery of society. Action on behalf of justice and participation in the transformation of the world is a constitutive element of preaching the gospel.

The Parish of the Risen Christ in Smokey Mountain exemplifies these ideals. A real belief in God requires solidarity with the poor. This serves to ease the poor's undeserved suffering by establishing *sedaqah* (justice) and *mishpat* (judgment). The church is living out its faith in God by coming alongside and working within the communities of the poor, helping them to help themselves.

While the main work in Smokey Mountain centers on material help, the most important goal is to evoke a sense of dignity and worth in each resident. Only by helping each individual feel loved and worthy is it possible to create a community. Once the community is formed, however, it is from within this community that faith is lived, deepened and celebrated in love. Only the poor have the power to truly help themselves and shape their own destiny. To encourage growth and development, this aspect of their faith must not be taken away. Instead, we should encourage the poor to develop this power.

For true change to occur, we must attend to the structures in society that make our feeding programs necessary, and confront the social structures that have turned the world into an individualistic, consumer society, instead of burying ourselves in religious practices to escape confronting the roots of suffering in the world.

Organizing for Community

From a presentation by Kenneth L. Luscombe, co-director of the Office of Urban Advance (OUA), a department of World Vision International responsible for the development of community organizations throughout the urban Third World. In this capacity, OUA has helped develop 28 grassroots community organizations in 21 cities. Rev. Luscombe is a Baptist minister from Melbourne, Australia. He currently makes his home near Los Angeles, USA.

Building community is an economic way of restating the heart of World Vision's mission in partnership with the poor, namely, "transformational development that is community-based." But what does building community actually mean?

Community is about people; people living within a specific area, sharing common ties and interacting with one another. Community is built when the conditions are right for creative interaction around issues of common concern by people who share a sense of connectedness and belonging. It is people working together to create the kind of environment they want to live in. This is taken for granted in communities of wealth and privilege, but not so in communities of the poor.

Building community, therefore, is essentially the task and prerogative of the people whose lives are invested in that community's future. This is an important point because too often, development work among the poor has been little more than outsider agencies doing things for people. In this case, the metaphor of "building" has been quite literally translated into the tangible construction of homes, schools, clinics and so forth.

But whenever people are unable to participate in the important decisions affecting their lives and community, they are rendered powerless. And it is powerlessness that ultimately destroys people and communities. This suggests that a more appropriate image for the metaphor of "building community" is energizing the process of self-determination, in the sense of building up the people. The term often used today to identify this process is "empowerment."

Building community by empowering people

Empowerment happens when people who are without power begin to speak, decide and act for themselves, when those without power insist in power sharing with the powerful, when people recover the God-given dignity of being human. In other words, empowerment is expressed through the values that give meaning to life: justice, equality and dignity.

Building community by empowering people is an approach to development particularly suited to urban areas. Here the need for community is paramount. Visit any major city of the world today and you will feel the relentless press of humanity. It is as if a floodgate had been lifted somewhere, releasing a surging mass of displaced humanity to swill over the city, filling every nook and cranny of unused and uncontested space. This surging mass becomes the urban poor, the crowd and the crowded. And in this swirling flood of humanity, all seems fluid, rootless and disorganized. But the city has another side. There is raw vitality in the press and bustle of the crowd, for the city also attracts those who aspire to a better way of life, appealing to their hopes and dreams and tapping into their energies of body, mind and spirit. Many achieve their dreams. But many more do not. They join the growing number of the disenchanted, dispossessed, powerless and defeated who shrink back into the anonymous recesses of the city.

In recent years, World Vision International's Office of Urban Advance has been involved in community building in selected slums, squatter camps and shanty-towns in cities of the Two-Thirds World. The approach of the Urban Advance has been that of community organization. The basic premise of this approach is that urban social problems exist when people cannot participate in any significant way in the major decisions affecting their lives, or feel powerless to address effectively the major concerns of their community. This finds expression in the two principles of community organizing: that the people of the community are the one's best able to identify and address the problems of the community; and that people can act most powerfully in addressing community problems when they act collectively.

The critical key: the community organizer

The critical key to the practice of community organization is not a program or a project but a person: the community organizer. The organizer enters the community as an enabler whose goal is to see people emerge from their powerlessness to self-determination through working together. They are "agents of change" or, with different imagery, "midwives" in the birth of the empowered community. Typically, the organizer will work with the community so that an organization of that community emerges through which the people have an active voice with and beyond that community. During this time, the organizer will seek to foster the growth of other important aspects of community appropriate to the different stages of development through which the people move in the maturing of their growth into community.

What are the characteristics of community that are being built up in the lives of the urban poor through community organization? These become apparent as we describe the activity of the community organizer at each step of the organizing process.

The community organizing process begins with the selection of a specific community. In most cases, this will be a parochial community identified by some obvious geographical or territorial boundaries. Community is understood at this stage as "neighborhood," within which the people share at least the commonality of proximity. A good deal of preparation lies behind this selection, and often the organizer will be invited into the community by a group, such as church leaders, who represent the interests of the community in some way.

After arriving in the community, the organizer begins to put together an understanding of the community by listening to the stories of a wide number of people, and to their definition of the basic issues of the community. So too the organizer tunes in to the special experiences and everyday social interactions that make up the "community consciousness" of the people, a consciousness that forms the invisible symbolic boundaries that mark out more decisively than geography the contours of the community. Unless the organizer steps inside this mythic identity of the community—that is, the ways the people think about themselves and the meanings they attach to their community—he or she will never "connect." Understanding what makes the community "tick," however, provides an opportunity to gather the people to address the matters of importance that they have identified.

A significant step forward in community organizing is achieved when people are brought together to address the issues they have defined as crucial to their development. The organizer forms coalitions based on the expressed self-interest of the people in achieving change in areas of mutual concern. Self-interest is at the heart of human motivation. When people feel deeply about something they are most likely to act to make a difference. Community happens when people feel mutually supported in their resolve to make a difference on matters of significance to their well-being. A sense of purpose and common resolve builds the confidence of the people, and gives them a structure through which to do something about what they believe. Since there are differences among people and what is important to them, so there are a variety of coalitions. Coalitions are a form of intermediary community–somewhere between the primary group of the family and the larger formal community organization.

Commitment to common goals

Community is found in the context of commitment to common goals. Once the organizer has gathered people into coalitions they begin to address those concerns through a process of action and reflection. The wellspring for action and reflection is the refusal to accept things "the way they are," as if this were a final statement about the way people should think and act. It is an act of "civil disbelieving."

The people begin to act, taking small and measured steps together as they gain the confidence for more substantial actions. And with every step into action the people join in reflection. They reflect upon the significance of their actions, and the further steps their actions demand. And along the way, they dig deeper and deeper into the resources of their common life. Values are surfaced, clarified, owned and tested to new depths as conflicts within and without refine the commitments of the group.

This is the context in which the organizer will look for those profound and "transforming" moments in the experience of the community when ultimate matters are at stake. In the midst of the struggle for freedom, self-determination and dignity, the life-denying powers of the vested interests and the status quo will surely rise up to ridicule the efforts of those who would change the order of things. At such times, the community and its members face the moment of truth. Confronting the enemy within and without takes an act of courage and commitment. But it takes something more. It takes faith: faith in the meaningfulness of life, faith in the worthwhileness of the struggle for justice and dignity, faith in the capacity of the human community to realize what is true and right and good. At some point, the organizer will help the people reflect on the adequacy of their vision of life and the foundational values by which this vision is grounded.

As a Christian, I would want to add a brief footnote to the above. Poverty brings death. The Spirit brings life. Building community is joining in the Spirit's birthing of new life into community through the overcoming of death and all that leads to it. The empowerment of the poor is not just a noble idea thought up by good and charitable people. It is no less than the advent of God's Spirit bringing life where it really counts. It is the Spirit, however, conceived in human terms, that ultimately births community.

In due course, the organizer will bring the coalitions of the community together to form a community organization. The energies of the coalitions now turn from mutual self-interest to enlightened community interest and beyond. The community organization builds on the experiences of solidarity and support that flow through the coalitions as they begin to address as one the larger social picture.

The "people power" of community organizing

We can see the "people power" of community organizing in the following stories. Twenty-seven community-based businesses have been created in Nairobi, Kenya. The government was successfully pressured to build 2,000 homes and rebuild the entire physical infrastructure of a slum in Madras, India. Slum community organizations in Belo Horizonte, Brazil, joined with non-governmental organizations to successfully pressure government policy and practices regarding the defense and advocacy of Belo's street children. In Dhaka, Bangladesh, a majority of urban slum occupants successfully used their newly learned capacity to read and write to press for social change. More important than these accomplishments, however, was the building of strong communities of the urban poor. Permanent organizations have been created in each slum by which the people continue to make and carry out decisions on the quality of their life together, and in which they keep on identifying and developing new leadership among slum residents.

Community organization is a thoroughgoing, empowerment-based approach to building community. The process of community organizing addresses all the varied nuances of "community." It begins with the delineation of community as living space, it draws the people together into coalitions of concern, where the community takes on issues of solidarity and common purpose. In the process of addressing specific issues, the members of the coalitions address the question of values, commitments and the deep structures of the religious vision of life.

The community, empowered through corporate action, becomes the vehicle for social change. People once caught in the cycles of despair can move step-by-step from private isolation to public involvement, from self-survival to enlightened self-interest, from powerlessness to the power and freedom of new life.

National Urban Ministries Network

From a presentation by Kinmoth Jefferson, who was the executive secretary of Urban Ministries for the United Methodist Church (USA) at the time of the Ruschlikon consultation. Rev. Jefferson lives in New York City, USA.

The Methodist Church in the USA developed from an urban center, and much of its history is apparent in the development of the cities. Missions itself arose out of a movement of inner city neighborhoods forming together to provide for the physical and spiritual needs of its own.

The National Urban Ministries (NUM) Network of the General Board of Global Ministries is a structure of the United Methodist Church (USA). It is sponsored by the Office of Urban Ministries and works closely with the Parish Ministries Program Management Unit and other units of the National Division. It also works closely with the new "Urban Ministries Initiative: Shalom and Community," which seeks to address "the massive deterioration of the spiritual and social fabric of communities across the United States."

The NUM Network's effort is organized around three program directions:. urban mission development, urban church development with an emphasis on urban church revitalization (this is vitally related in outreach to communities—local, regional, national and global) in the name of Jesus Christ, and urban community development. All three programs are designed to address visible decay occurring in the neighborhoods in terms of spiritual growth and communities. The social fabric across the countries has begun to erode. NUM has, therefore, developed its programs to help combat this.

The first program direction in NUM is urban mission development. Urban mission development is comprised of six goals. Goal one calls for the development of metropolitan ministry coordinating agencies. The second goal seeks to network urban ministries at the jurisdictional and national levels. Once the network is established, the third goal is to strengthen the annual conference and national division linkages. The development of an ecumenical/inter-faith joint strategy is sought as the fourth goal. This goal is also concerned with developing a set of action objectives. The fifth goal focuses on support for the Native American Urban Ministries Initiative. Finally, the development of urban mission requires support for the General Council of Bishops' Initiative on Substance Abuse. The combination of these six goals is designed to aid in the development of urban mission and therefore help cultivate a greater spiritual depth and sense of community in the urban area.

The second program direction, urban church development, places major priority on developing and strengthening local urban-ethnic, minority churches. It also emphasizes developing and strengthening the urban congregations composed of both poor and "working class" constituencies as well as those situated in urban, changing communities and small membership churches. With the strengthening and development of these churches and congregations, the church will have the base to work for strong neighborhoods.

Another priority in urban church development is the development and strengthening of urban cooperative parish ministries, including "shared facilities." This will allow different congregations access to resources that are otherwise not available. With this access, churches can grow and institute programs they may not normally have been able to do. A fourth priority in urban church development is to emphasize and encourage the development and strengthening of missional commitments and involvements of "stronger" churches in central city and suburbia. When a community can send out its own missionaries to the field this is a final indicator of spiritual growth, and should therefore be encouraged.

The third program direction is urban community development. The strategy is to develop and strengthen church involvement in urban community organizing and urban community economic development. This strengthens the church's commitment to its neighborhood as it begins to invest in the community's growth and revitalization. The next step is to develop and strengthen advocacy programs and coalitions in major areas of urban concern. This works on limiting the social problems in the city by taking a hands-on approach to their eradication. These can include but are not limited to: racial justice, economic justice, justice in the area of immigration and refugee concerns, criminal justice, access to affordable health care, environmental issues and appropriate urban-related public policy.

Urban Mission Among the Poor:
An Incarnational Approach

From a presentation by Viv Grigg, the director of Urban Leadership Foundation (ULF) and coordinator of the Cities Track for the AD2000 movement. He was a church planter and community development worker in Manila and Calcutta for many years before assuming leadership of the ULF. Mr. Grigg is a New Zealand Baptist and lives in Auckland, New Zealand.

Luke 4:18 serves as the theological basis for ministry with the poor. Ministering to the poor began at Pentecost, in the anointing and empowering of the Spirit. Today, among the urban poor many grassroots types of organizations have developed. Their effectiveness is minimal, however, without the involvement of the churches.

There are two important goals for Christians to own. The first is the elimination of poverty; the second is the living out of Christ's prayer, "Thy kingdom come on earth." In order for these two goals to occur, a community of people living among the poor and under the authority of the kingdom must exist. Consequently, the only way to develop churches is through preaching accompanied by signs and wonders. Economic projects, in and of themselves, are not sufficient.

The church must not only preach the Word of God but it must simultaneously respond to the physical needs, spirit possession, sickness and injustice so prevalent in cities. For churches to grow, they must develop a system of discipleship alongside their work of economic development. Neglecting the discipling and only emphasizing the economic programs results in a lack of development, with a greater likelihood that the gospel will be neglected and remain unpreached.

If the church is to bring the Word of God to the slums, a movement of workers committed to living among the poor as nondestitute poor, living simply and developing the church and community from within must occur. If people go into the slums and act as individuals, they will not be able to survive. Instead, they must become part of a community of six to twelve workers working side-by-side to advance the kingdom. The importance of community must be greatly emphasized.

The question to ask when working with the poor becomes not how do we as outsiders help them. Rather, the question must be, "How can the poor help themselves and each other?" Education, credit co-ops, land right movements, movements of churches among the educated elite are all part of the development of a solution to help end the oppression of the poor. The most important thing to remember, however, is that the solution lies not in individuals, but in the effort of the community as a whole.

Urban Ministry in the Coptic Orthodox Church

From a presentation by Maurice Assad, the associate general secretary of the Middle East Council of churches in Cairo, Egypt, specializing in urban work. He is a member of the Coptic Orthodox Church and makes his home in Cairo, Egypt.

The cities in Egypt began to grow and develop as the people of Egypt, for various reasons, were pulled away from their homelands. They flocked to the cities, which were considered the center of worship and the location of power. This happened as cities began to grow and become both bigger and stronger. As a result, the government began to centralize its position in the cities. So cities have greatly increased in size and a shift of importance from rural to urban areas has now occurred. For many Egyptians today, the city has become the symbol of hope as many migrants dream of an improved quality of life.

In Egypt, the population increases by one million every seven months. This poses tremendous problems for cities as pressures on resources and infrastructure are continually strained. Education, health care, streets and sewer systems are all examples of parts of the infrastructure that are being stretched.

For the Coptic Orthodox Church in Egypt, the focus is on worship, witnessing and learning. The liturgy of the church serves to bring together the whole people of God (the *koinonia*). Faith and life intermix in the Coptic Church in the Eucharist. Thus, the Eucharist becomes the bond of unity among the members of the church.

Schools play a vital role in the Coptic Orthodox community and offer an education to both Christian and Muslim children. The 1930s and 1940s marked the beginning of the "Sunday School" movement in Egypt. Sunday schools consequently play a vital and important role in the renewal movement and life of the church. The Coptic Orthodox Church also participates in weekly biblical teachings by Pope Shenouda and other church leaders. For Bible studies, the congregation comes with questions, and the bishop acts as facilitator. The church recognizes and affirms the role of the Holy Spirit as the ultimate and true teacher.

The urban family of the church is another important element in the Coptic Orthodox tradition. The Coptic church has begun recently to feel the strains of urban problems in the congregation, and has taken some solid steps to work in the direction of improving the current situation. Classes on marriage and new life together have commenced in order to help the members of the congregation maintain their focus on God.

Generally, however, the Coptic church is recognized as an apostolic church of the poor.

A Missionary Parish at the
Edge of the Largest City of the World

From a presentation by Alfonso Navarro, the pastor and leader of La Parroquia de la Resurreccion; in this ministry, he has developed a strong evangelistic and social activist effort that mobilizes the poor and the powerful to work for the transformation of their city. Fr. Navarro lives in Mexico City, Mexico.

In August 1981, the resurrection began for the people of a rapidly expanding squatter settlement on the outskirts of Mexico City. There, the Parish of the Resurrection came into being as a missionary effort of the Roman Catholic Church. The effort began with the 7,500 families (a total of about 40,000 people) living there. These were people who were unemployed, subemployed or living on a minimal salary. They had migrated from different corners of the country, "parachuters" (as labeled by the government) who suddenly appeared overnight (500 more families in just one weekend, for example).

The parish was a "missionary extension field" of the Center of Evangelization, an effort that had been developing during the previous ten years south of Mexico City, and close to the university campus. Two thousand people were coming every week to attend a three-day evangelization event, and from that encounter formed small communities to sustain their growth in the faith. More than 1,000 people every year intentionally responded to the evangelization experience. This has continued until the present day. And it is from this Center of Evangelization that the personnel and material resources have been mobilized over a decade to sustain the development of the parish in the squatter settlement.

The Parish of the Resurrection is the pilot project of a pastoral model for parishes and Catholic schools. This

project is named SINE (Systematic Integral New Evangelization). SINE, as a model for ministry, now extends
beyond the parish into 13 countries and more than 500
parishes in the USA, Latin America and Spain.

"Evangelization" is the absolute priority of this
model—the joyful proclamation of a living Jesus, inviting
each person to have a personal encounter with him, experience salvation and new life, and receive baptism in the
Holy Spirit. The approach is an "integral" holistic effort,
built upon the recognition that evangelization must con-
sist of more than the proclamation of the word (*kerygma*),
but must include the sustaining of community (*koinonia*),
the worship of God (*leitourgia*) and the substantive
addressing of social concerns (*diakonia*). It is "new" in that
it is directed toward nominal Catholics, and it is "systematic" because it follows an organized plan for the transformation of parishes.

SINE is built around seven elements:

- ❖ Outreach to the nominal Catholics in the parish
- ❖ Evangelization encounter through a retreat
- ❖ Small communities and parishes as a communion
  of communities
- ❖ Catechetical and biblical teaching
- ❖ Celebration of the sacraments
- ❖ Social action; and
- ❖ Apostolic involvement of every member of the
  congregation in the work of transformation.

The work of SINE is accomplished in this way. The
parish is divided into geographical sectors, subsectors,
streets and homes. Thus, the Parish of the Resurrection is
divided into eight sectors, with from 600 to 1,000 families
in each sector, 120 families in each subsector and 20 families to a "street." Every person and every family in that
parish is included.

Consecrated and spiritually committed lay people—four to six to a sector—visit door-to-door all year long, relating to people, learning of their issues and needs and their religious and social concerns. But most important is sharing with each family the Good News of God's redemptive love in Christ, inviting them to make a personal response to accept Jesus as Savior and Lord, and turn to God in repentance and conversion.

When a person or family responds to this invitation, they meet in a "gathering house" with others who have also been "touched;" there, they are nurtured and supported by the parish workers. From the gathering house, they are asked to make an "evangelization retreat." At the retreat, they experience the work of Christ in their midst through the biblically-based teaching (*kerygma*), the dynamic and Spirit-filled worship (liturgy), the building of a life in supportive community (*koinonia*) and in identification with and involvement in the social action of the parish. A wide spectrum of possible retreats are available: full weekend retreats, a daily meeting for three weeks, a weekly session for four months, or a combination of these alternatives.

After participation in the evangelization retreat, people become involved in the life and ministry of their parish. In street, sector and parish gatherings, people gather for three hours every week for praise, study of the Word, spiritual edification and social solidarity. They also select an area of ministry or social action in which they will be involved. This includes both geographical sectors and ministry fields.

The geographical sectors are ministries dealing with the holistic development of that specific geographical area—a comprehensive concern with the entire quality of life of that neighborhood, including the social needs that are addressed or for which the community is mobilized through these ongoing gatherings. The ministry fields deal with specific social needs or issues to which all the people in a gathering have committed themselves. Ministries that groups are currently carrying out are family issues, the youth, the sick, the elderly, rehabilitation for drug addicts, alcoholism, gangs, prostitutes, homosexuality, evangelization and so on. The sectors are geographic in nature and integrative in intent; the ministry fields are functional and specialist in nature. The social work is then coordinated by a parish council, which is made up of all the heads of all the sectors and ministries.

Urban Development Project

From a presentation by Jember Teferra, the coordinator of the Integrated Urban Development Project, a major community development work in a slum of Addis Ababa, Ethiopia. With her husband and some members of her family, she was a political prisoner after the coup against Haile Selassie. She is a member of the Coptic Church, is active in evangelical church circles and lives in Addis Ababa with her husband and family.

I would like to share with you the work of the Integrated Holistic Approach Urban Development Project in Woreda 3, *Kebeles* 30, 41, 42 and 43, a large and extremely destitute slum located in Addis Ababa, Ethiopia. It is the first development project located in that slum. When the project began, Emmanuel Baptist Church functioned as the overseer and channeled funds for the project.

The work of this project began in June 1989. It targeted those groups of people who were considered to be the poorest of the poor. Some of these people groups include: self-employed women, children, old people, the disabled and disadvantaged, and the unemployed or "self-employed" male who has a low level of income.

The Integrated Urban Development Project has several objectives. These goals are to improve the quality of life through a community-based, integrated holistic approach and to leave the project communities self-sufficient with sustainable means to maintain the development process after the project phases out. The latter goal is important to develop so that the project does not die when the sponsors and supporters leave. In order for this to happen people must be conscientized into changing their overwhelming attitudes of hopelessness.

Another of the project's goals is to create a social awareness in the community and thereby enhance participation in development programs. By making the people more aware of what is going on around them and the prevalent hopelessness, they are put into a position that allows them to respond to their own needs.

The project consists of three components: 1) the physical upgrading of the area; 2) community development, including income generation and health care; and 3) an ongoing appeal for donations to help support the project. These three components are designed as a triangle to break the cycle of poverty and help improve the quality of life evident in the four *kebeles* (Woreda 3) of Addis Ababa.

What the First World Church Can Learn from Third World Urban Christians

From a presentation by Robert Linthicum, the editor of this book. His background is outlined in the credits section of this book.

Since I began work with World Vision International's Office of Urban Advance in 1985, it has been my privilege to interact with many urban pastors throughout

Asia, Africa and Latin America. This has included personal visits, working in ministry alongside them, leading pastors' conferences and workshops, and preaching or teaching in many churches. Out of the ongoing interaction with these urban pastors, I have observed several significant differences between the Third World urban church and the First World church. Those differences hold transforming potential for the North American and European churches.

What, then, can the First World city church learn from Third World urban Christianity?

Being is more important than doing

I was scheduled to preach at the Ngong Presbyterian Church in the Mathare Valley slum of Nairobi, Kenya. The service began in the usual Presbyterian manner—cold enough to ice skate down the central aisle. But then the singing began. The 700 people assembled for one of that church's three worship services that day began to sing in the unique style of east Africa. Back and forth the singing went from caller to congregation. Soon people began to clap; then they began to sway. Next, they started stamping their feet with the rhythm. Then worshippers stepped out into the aisle. And soon that congregation of 700 was dancing in sheer delight before the Lord!

Unusual? Not really—for these Presbyterians were living out the injunction of their catechism that taught them that "humanity's chief end is to glorify God and to enjoy God forever."

North American and European Christians mistakenly assume that the way to build a church is through programs. Our churches are full of committees meeting to plan projects—from selecting church school curricula to the planning of a church social, from developing a food distribution project for the hungry to devising an evange-

listic campaign. We organize through programming. And we are rewarded for such effort with overly committed people, jammed church calendars and burned-out workers. There must be a better way.

There is—and it is found in those Third World congregations that have avoided modeling themselves on the First World church. In churches like the Ngong Presbyterian Church, Christians have discovered that the basis of church life must not lie in programming, but in celebration. What they perceive the church is about is the task of building and sustaining Christian community. It is Christian community that forms the backbone of their church life. It is the foundation upon which all worship, Christian nurture, support of one another, evangelism and social activism are built.

Relationships are given a higher priority than production. What you are in relation to each other is more important than what you accomplish. This is a style of being church that First World Christians desperately need to experience.

Identify with the people

We gathered in the shack of a Christian worker in a slum in Jakarta, Indonesia. This man and his family were involved in a profound ministry to those slum dwellers, enabling them to fight exploitation by large corporations housed in a complex across the road. The poor, not able to stand up to the powerful before, now successfully insisted on safety and on decent employee benefits. I asked this college graduate, "What was the secret of such phenomenal success among the poor?" He answered with just five words: "We moved in among them!"

Many Third World urban churches are committed to incarnating themselves in the neighborhoods in which they are placed, with both the pastors and the congregations identifying with and casting their lot with the residents. This, I have discovered, is particularly true of Pentecostal churches, whose pastors and people have moved throughout the Third World into the worst slums where they concentrate equally on ministries of evangelism and social activism while undergoing considerable sacrifice in the process.

One of the unique manifestations of this incarnational approach to ministry is the pastors' willingness to sacrifice financial security. It is unusual in the Third World to meet full-time pastors. Pastoral support to congregations often occurs not by having one pastor serving full-time in a church, but by the formation of a team of three to six part-time pastors who share pastoral service to a church. Notably absent from such team effort is the sense of burnout and over-extension found in so many First World pastors.

Because of such situations, pastors often serve for little or no pay and churches are freed to invest in mission. Congregations choose mission advances, not by asking whether they can afford it (they never can), but whether God is calling them into such commitment to the poor. The results are congregations liberated from fiscal intimidation and programming stultification.

Know you can take the people no further than you are willing to go yourself

In Madras, India, I was providing leadership to the first Indian urban workshop in which I had been involved. As we reviewed the agenda, I could sense unrest in the room. Something was wrong with that schedule.

I discovered soon enough what it was. I had allotted only one hour for lunch instead of two. When I asked why they felt they needed so much time, one of them answered, "We need time to feed our souls as well as our bodies."

Initially, I thought that an excuse. I soon discovered that it was not. After lunch, I observed most of the participants spending time in silence, reflection or quietly reading their Bibles. They were, in fact, feeding their souls.

A pastor can take his or her congregation spiritually no further than that pastor is willing to go himself or herself. You cannot introduce people to dimensions of Christ you have not experienced. And it has been my privilege to discover, over and over again, how keenly aware of this reality Third World urban pastors are—and how earnestly they seek after a deeper relationship with Christ.

There is, with almost every Third World urban pastor I have met, a hunger after God. They seek to build a spirituality that is truly effective support to pastor and people alike as they live out the gospel in their city. This includes a spirituality adequate to sustain and direct them as they confront the systems and structures of their cities.

Coupled with a commitment to a functional spirituality is the search for an urban biblical theology. Perhaps the outstanding characteristic of the Third World urban church is its commitment to think theologically and biblically about its ministry. The largest gathering of Protestant and evangelical urban pastors in Bogota's history occurred in 1987; that gathering was to attend a five-day workshop that dealt only with the exploration of an urban biblical theology. I have yet to participate in an urban conference in the Third World in which biblical reflection about the city is not a primary emphasis.

Justice is more important than service

I was visiting with a Methodist pastor and the director of that denomination's community center in a slum in one of Brazil's largest cities. They told me of how poor people in that slum became tired of living in such deplorable conditions. With the church's encouragement, the people petitioned the government for free land on which they could build their homes. They had received assurances from Habitat for Humanity that the people would be assisted in their financing and building of these homes. For two years, the government put off these petitioners. Finally, it agreed they could have the land if they showed up at the site on a certain day to claim it.

When this small group arrived to claim the land, they found there were about three times as many people as there were parcels of land to be distributed—and each had been promised a parcel! Of course, the inevitable happened. The people fell to arguing and the government stepped in to maintain order. Insisting the poor had proven themselves once again unable to manage such decisions, the government reclaimed the land.

In the face of such injustice, the church and its community center joined forces with those poor people to battle the government for that land. They finally won after another year of struggle. "But we learned a valuable lesson from that incident," the pastor told me. "It is not enough to serve people's needs. You have to stand with them when they try to better their own lives. And sometimes that means fighting for what is just."

Whether it is a Baptist church in Harare, Zimbabwe, a Pentecostal church in Bogota, Colombia, or a coalition of pastors working among prostitutes in Bombay, India, there are two essential themes I hear Christians stressing repeatedly as they undertake ministry among the urban poor and powerless.

First, they insist that the work of the church must move beyond ministries of mercy and compassion to deal with the systemic and substantive issues that create and maintain poverty in their cities. The increasing focus of such ministry is not simply the feeding of the hungry or distribution of clothing or caring for children. The focus for such ministry is for practical, small scale economic development and people-empowering community organization in which the poor take charge of their own situations.

Second, there is a steadily growing concern on the part of urban pastors and workers that any church strategy must involve the poor not as objects of the ministry of the church, but as subjects. Urban programs increasingly involve the participation of the poor in reflection and action in both the analysis of the issues and the determination of the project or action to address those issues. Self- and community-determination are as important as the results (i.e., the process is as important to them as is the product).

Life in community, celebration, identification with the poor, discovery of an urban spirituality and theology, a commitment to justice for the poor and participation of the poor as subjects are some of the developing trends in Asian, African and Latin American urban churches today. What is occurring is an increasingly biblical, spiritual, social, political and economic sophistication on the part of Third World pastors, churches and parachurch organizations. Perhaps the First World church can learn from such trends, and discover for themselves " a more excellent way" of being church in the city.

Appendixes

Appendix One: Bibliography

Summary reports have been compiled by Michael Eastman ("A Risk Worth Taking"), Grant McClung ("Report and Reflections") and Robert Linthicum ("Report on the International Urban Consultation"). Each report has been used in developing this book.

Appendix Two:
Participants at the Ruschlikon Event

Name	Location	Affiliation	Mission Agency
Abraham, Viju	Bombay, India	Pentecostal	Urban Mission Center
Asher, Moshe ben	San Francisco, USA	Jewish Reformed	Organize Training Center
Assad, Maurice	Cairo, Egypt	Coptic	Middle East Council of Churches
Aykazan, Vicken	Geneva, Switzerland	Orthodox	World Council of Churches
Bakke, Ray	Chicago, USA	Baptist	International Urban Associates
Beltran, Benigno	Manila, Philippines	Roman Catholic	Smokey Mountain Parish
Berry, Dave	Leicester, UK	Church of England	Bd. of Mission/Social Response
Conrath, Wally	Philadelphia, USA	Salvation Army	Salvation Army
Cook, Suzan J.	New York USA	Baptist	Mariner's Temple
Devasundaram, Alex	Bangalore, India	Church of N. India	Industrial Mission
Eastman, Michael	London, UK	Baptist/Pent.	Frontier Youth Trust
Ellis, Elward	College Park, USA	Baptist	Destiny Movement, Inc.
Foster, Alan	Melbourne, Australia	Anglican	St. Albans Anglican Parish
French, David	Chicago, USA	Baptist	Seminary Consortium for Urban Pastoral Education (SCUPE)
Githumbi, Stephen	Nairobi, Kenya	Presbyterian	World Vision Kenya
Green, Clifford	Hartford, U.S.A.	Lutheran	Public Policy Center
Grigg, Viv	New Zealand	Pentecostal	Urban Leadership Program
Hathaway, Brian	Auckland, NZ	Open Brethren	Te Atatu Bible Chapel
Jefferson, Kim	New York, USA	United Methodist	Urban Ministry Desk

Name	Location	Affiliation	Mission Agency
Linthicum, Robert	Los Angeles, USA	Presbyterian	Office of Urban Advance- World Vision Int'l.
Luscombe, Ken	Melbourne, Australia	Baptist	Office of Urban Advance- World Vision Int'l.
Maroney, Jimmy	Richmond, USA	Southern Baptist	Foreign Mission Board
McAlpine, Tom	Los Angeles, USA	Presbyterian	Urban Evangelism- MARC
McClung, Grant	Cleveland, USA	Church of God	Church of God World Missions
McGibbon, Carol A.	Chicago, USA	Baptist	Seminary Consortium for Urban Pastoral Education (SCUPE)
McMahon, Dorothy	Melbourne, Australia	Uniting Church	Commission for Mission
Messick, Fred	Los Angeles, USA	Episcopal	World Vision United States
Molebatsi, Caesar	Orlando, S. Africa	Pentecostal	Youth Alive Ministries
Nandjui, Simon	Abidjan, Ivory Coast	Methodist	Prison Fellowship
Navarro, Alfonso	Mexico City, Mexico	Roman Catholic	Parish of the Resurrection
Sauca, Ioan	Bucharest, Romania	Orthodox	Romanian Patriarchate
Shane, John	Nairobi, Kenya	Presbyterian	SIM Urban Center
Smith, Ernie	Melbourne, Australia	Roman Catholic	Sacred Heart Parish Mission
Smith, Glenn	Montreal, Canada	Brethren	Christian Direction
Teferra, Jember	Addis Ababa,. Ethiopia	Coptic	Evangelical Int'l Urban Development Project
Terzic, Dragan	Doboj, Yugoslavia	Orthodox	Serbian Orthodox Church
Ujvarosy, Stephen	Chicago, USA	Evangelical	International Urban Associates
Vincent, John	Sheffield, UK	Methodist	Urban Theology Unit

The Rev. Mr. Stewart Culbard of Northampton, UK, an urban Baptist minister, was contract staff for the consultation. Also present as spouses of participants were Marlene Linthicum, Joy Luscombe, Sandra Messick, Chumi Molebatsi and Mrs. Nandjui, all of whom were invited to participate fully in the consultation.

Appendix Three

Steering and Programming Committees
of the International Urban Ministry Network

Moderator
Robert C. Linthicum (USA)
Partners in Urban Transformation
3300 Wilshire Boulevard
Los Angeles, CA 90010 USA

Vice Moderator
Dorothy McRae-McMahon (Australia)
Commission for Mission
The Uniting Church in Australia
Box E266, St. James P.O.
Sydney NSW 2000, Australia

Secretary-Treasurer
Stephen Ujvarosy (USA)
Partners in Urban Transformation
3300 Wilshire Boulevard
Los Angeles, CA 90010 USA
(new organization and address: see Linthicum)

Maurice Assad (Egypt)
Middle East Council of Churches
P.O. Box 2238, Horeya
Heliopolis 11361, Cairo, Egypt

Ray Bakke (USA)
International Urban Associates
5151 North Clark, 2nd Floor
Chicago, IL 60640 USA

Fr. Benigno Beltran (Philippines)
Sambayanan ng Muling Pagkabuhay
P.O. Box 2036
Tondo, Manila, Philippines

David Berry (UK)
Board of Mission and Social Responsibility
Diocese of Leicester
278 East Park Road
Leicester LE5 5AY, England

Suzan Johnson Cook (USA)
Mariners' Temple Baptist Church
3 Henry Street
New York, NY 10038

Michael Eastman (UK)
Frontier Youth Trust
130 City Road
London, EC1V 2NJ, England

Kenneth Luscombe (Australia)
World Vision International
121 E. Huntington Drive
Monrovia, CA 91016 USA

Grant McClung (USA)
Church of God World Missions
P.O. Box 8016
Cleveland, TN 37320-8016 USA

Carol Ann McGibbon (Canada)
Seminary Consortium for Urban
    Pastoral Education
200 N. Michigan, Suite 502
Chicago, IL 60601 USA

Caesar Molebatsi (South Africa)
Youth Alive Ministries
P.O. Box 129
1804 Orlando, South Africa

Simon Nandjui (Cote d'Ivoire)
2 rue Aristide Briand
74 100 Annemasse, France

Alfonso Navarro (Mexico)
Nueva Evangelizacion Integral
Kantunil 419
Pedregal de San Nicolas
14100 Mexico City, DF, Mexico

Ioan Sauca (Romania)
Romanian Orthodox Church
150 Route de Femey
P.O. Box 2100
1211 Geneva 2, Switzerland

Glenn Smith (Canada)
Christian Direction, Inc.
455 St. Antoine St., W. Room 602
Montreal, Quebec H2Z 1J1, Canada

Jeff Thindwa (Malawi)
World Vision of the United Kingdom
World Vision House
599 Avebury Blvd.
Central Milton Keynes
Bucks, MK9 3PG, England

John Vincent (UK)
Urban Theology Unit
210 Abbeyfield Road
Sheffield S4 7AZ, England

Congress Organizing Committee

Michael Eastman, Chair
Robert Linthicum
Grant McClung
Dorothy McRae-McMahon
Ioan Sauca
Stephen Ujvarosy

Urban Theologians International

Carol Ann McGibbon, Chair
Ray Bakke
Benigno Beltran
David Berry
Suzan Johnson Cook
Ken Luscombe
John Vincent

Publications Committee

Grant McClung, Chair
Robert Linthicum
Stephen Ujvarosy

Members of the All-Africa Planning Team

David K. Ashiko
World Vision Kenya
P.O. Box 50816
Nairobi, Kenya

Cecil Begbie
H.E.L.P. Ministries International
P.O. Box 38256
Gatesville, Capetown 7764, South Africa

Michael Eastman
Frontier Youth Trust
130 City Road
London BC1V 2N5, England

David N. Gichung'wa
Scripture Union - Kenya
P.O. Box 40717
Nairobi, Kenya

Osbome Joda-Mbewe
World Vision Malawi
P.O. Box 2050
Blantyre, Malawi

Grace Kaiso
World Vision Uganda
P.O. Box 5319
Kampala, Uganda

Crispus Karingithi
World Vision Kenya
P.O. Box 50816
Nairobi, Kenya

Charles Kibicho Kariuki
St. Andrew's Presbyterian Church
P.O. Box 41282
Nairobi, Kenya

Robert Linthicum
Partners in Urban Transformation
3300 Wilshire Blvd.
Los Angeles, CA 90010 USA

Thomas Malande
Scripture Union - Kenya
P.O. Box 40717
Nairobi, Kenya

Celestin Musekura
Missions Urbaines et Liaison, Rwanda
c/o P.O. Box 60875
Nairobi, Kenya

Isaya Guy Otemba
United Bible Societies
African Regional Service Centre
P.O. Box 42726
Nairobi, Kenya

Janet Prest Talbot
Anchor House (YMCA)
82 St. Andrew's Street
Durban 4001, South Africa

Stuart Talbot
D'Urban Network
21 St. Andrew's Street
Durban 4001, South Africa

Jember Teferra
Integrated Urban Development Project
P.O. Box 1296
Addis Ababa, Ethiopia

Stephen Ujvarosy
Partners in Urban Transformation
3300 Wilshire Blvd.
Los Angeles, CA 90010 USA
(new organization and address: see Robert Linthicum)

MARC

Bringing you key resources on the world mission of the church

MARC books and other publications support the work of MARC (Mission Advanced Research and Communications Center), which is to inspire fresh vision and empower Christian mission among those who extend the whole gospel to the whole world.

Recent MARC titles include:

▶ *By Word, Work and Wonder*, Thomas H. McAlpine. Examines the question of holism in Christian mission and brings you several case studies from around the world that will push your thinking on this important topic. $15.95

▶ *Serving with the Poor in Asia: Cases in Holistic Ministry*, T. Yamamori, B. Myers and D. Conner, editors. Well-known mission leaders comment on cases in holistic mission presented from seven different Asian contexts. These cases and analyses help us better understand what a holistic witness to the gospel of Christ means today. $15.95

▶ *God So Loves the City: Seeking a Theology for Urban Mission*, Charles Van Engen and Jude Tiersma, editors. Experienced urban practitioners from around the world explore the most urgent issues facing those who minister in today's cities in search of a theology for urban mission. $21.95

▶ *Healing the Children of War*, Phyllis Kilbourn, editor. A handbook for Christians who desire to be of service to children who have suffered deep traumas as a result of war. $21.95

▶ *The Changing Shape of World Mission* by Bryant L. Myers. Presents in color graphs, charts and maps the challenge before global missions, including the unfinished task of world evangelization. Also available in color slides and over-heads—excellent for presentations!

Book..$ 5.95
Slides..$ 99.95
Overheads.......................................$ 99.95
Presentation Set *(one book, slides and overheads)* $175.00

Order Toll Free in USA: 1-800-777-7752
Visa and MasterCard accepted

MARC A division of World Vision International
121 E. Huntington Dr. • Monrovia • CA • 91016-3400

Ask for the MARC Newsletter and complete publications list